THE CONFIDENT COACH'S GUIDE
TO TEACHING BASKETBALL

THE CONFIDENT COACH'S GUIDE TO TEACHING BASKETBALL

Beverly Breton Carroll,

with John Carroll

THE LYONS PRESS
Guilford, Connecticut

An imprint of The Globe Pequot Press

The Lyons Press is an imprint of The Globe Pequot Press.

10 9 8 7 6 5 4 3 2 1

Printed in the United States of America

Designed by Stephanie Doyle

ISBN 1-59228-062-5

Library of Congress Cataloging-in-Publication Data is available on file.

For all who love the game of basketball

ACKNOWLEDGMENTS

To Tom McCarthy, who not only made producing this book possible, but a pleasure from start to finish;

To Jim Byrnes, whose unflagging enthusiasm and dedication to teaching young people basketball remains an inspiration;

To Dave Peterson, who has mastered holding practices where kids learn and have fun;

To Mary Jo Rulnick, who voluntarily went over this manuscript as if it were her own;

To Steve Lipofsky, who infused boundless patience into every photo minute;

And to Austin Carroll, who not only put up with several sessions of his opinionated parents trying to blend two visions into one, but supported the whole project, every step of the way—

Thank you one and all.

And additional thanks to our photo models for sharing their enjoyment of the game. Keep playing!

CONTENTS

FOREWORD

I am very lucky because I fell in love twice in my lifetime. At age 29, I met a beautiful and extremely intelligent woman who I fell head over heels for and married two years later. That woman is the author of this book, mother of my son Austin, and the person with whom I have shared the last 16 years. However, I fell in love at a very early age also. As memory serves me, I discovered the game of basketball somewhere around the age of 5, and promptly fell in love.

I love the game of basketball. I love the beauty and grace of it, the competitiveness of playing it. I have loved the challenge of pushing my body and mind to attempt new moves, higher, quicker and better. I have loved being a player, and after playing, I have loved coaching the game of basketball. Basketball has allowed me the opportunity over my lifetime to meet wonderful people, develop lifetime friends, and have some wonderful mentors. It has allowed me to get a better education than I probably would have had, travel the world playing and coaching, and to start right off in the world after college with a job. A job that I can say I love and enjoy going to every day.

I look at this game in a special way, and I think the game of basketball should be played a certain way. I have treated the game with great respect, and attempt to teach others to do the same. Every time I watch a game, teach or coach, I have tried to help young players understand the game the way I have been taught and studied the game. Now as I watch and study youth practices and games, I see a tremendous slippage in the fundamentals of the game. It hurts me to see the game I love becoming what I see. It was important to me to help write this book with Beverly to give young coaches and players an aid to use and refer to when practicing or working on their games. We have a lot of parents and young players with a lot of enthusiasm for the game but I feel they could use a guide to help them through their journey of teaching the game I love so much.

I have been lucky in my lifetime to have had several mentors guide me. Whether it was Tony Zotti, my next door neighbor and "second father" who had a court and hoop and allowed me to play at any hour of the day in his yard, and I mean any hour. This is where I fell in love with the game, imagined myself one-on-one versus John Havlicek and Jerry West, and developed an appreciation for how correctly the 1969 NY Knicks played the game. Or my ninth grade coach Lou Diparisi, who was without question the best coach I ever played for or learned from. Every young boy should be so lucky as to have a coach teach the fundamentals of the game the way Lou did. In college, I had two coaches, Dave Watkins, and Gene Evans. Dave recruited me and showed me an unbridled enthusiasm for the game while Gene was the elder statesman whose history and knowledge of the game are unparalleled. Gene has remained an unbelievable friend and mentor throughout my coaching days. I have been lucky to be coaching in college or the NBA since I graduated from college in 1977. Two people that helped me in that path were John Beecroft, who was a very good player at University of Pennsylvania in the 70's. In 1977, he took me under his wing and taught me how to teach, organize drills, and conduct a practice. And in 1982, I met a person that changed my life forever: P. J. Carlesimo. He hired me as an assistant coach at Seton Hall University in the Big East Conference. I spent seven years with him meeting more people than I could have ever imagined, recruiting all over the country, and getting a chance to be a coach in the NCAA National Championship game in 1989. I consider him to be the brother I never had, and what I have admired most about him from the day I met him is his honesty and integrity.

The above men I mentioned were formal mentors who I am forever in debt to for their help, guidance and friendship. However, there were also some important people closer to home. My Mom and Dad faithfully supported my love of the game of basketball by encouraging me to play, driving me wherever there was a game, and sitting through countless hours of a bouncing ball whether I was playing, or now, coaching. And my sisters rebounded for me when I was young (I still don't know why) and sat with my parents in the stands on numerous occasions (probably in disgust) watching my games.

These mentors, and my love of the game, have been a special gift. I believe I not only have a deep knowledge of the game of basketball but a passion for it. I hope that Beverly and I will be able in the following chapters to crystallize this for you and help you develop the ability to bring this knowledge to as many young people as possible. I pass this gift on now to you, and all the young people whose lives you will touch through this wonderful game of basketball.

John Carroll

INTRODUCTION

Practice doesn't make perfect.

So believes Celtics coach John Carroll, who has coached college and pro basketball in a career spanning more than 25 years. He is also the father of a 13-year-old son who plays on a championship Amateur Athletic Union (AAU) basketball team that he co-coaches, and the founder of All-Star Basketball Camps in Massachusetts where he coaches hundreds of kids from ages 7 through 16 every summer.

Practice does not make perfect.

But perfect practice does make perfect. This is the credo Coach Carroll lives his basketball life by. Years of experience have only strengthened his conviction that players need to learn the fundamentals of basketball. When players practice the correct fundamentals, repeatedly, until they become perfect habits, those players are the most prepared to meet an opponent that they can be. A player who's learned incorrect habits and techniques is going to be exponentially behind any player who has learned correct techniques. And teaching new habits to a player with bad habits is extremely difficult.

"I don't think anyone teaching young people basketball can go wrong using a guide of fundamentals," asserts Coach Carroll. "These fundamentals could be drilled from grade school through high school, and a coach would never be in the position of underteaching or undercoaching because so many young people are not exposed to fundamentals these days."

And that's what coaching is: Coaching is teaching.

A confident coach translates into confident players—confident that, in the speed of a game situation, they can rely on the skills drilled into their young bodies.

So read on. Light the flame. And let the practices begin!

Part I

THE FUNDAMENTALS

CHAPTER 1

COACHING YOUTH BASKETBALL

What is basketball? It's running, bouncing a ball, passing, and shooting a ball into a basket. Sounds simple.

From a spectator's viewpoint, maybe. Now let's look at basketball from a coach's viewpoint. It's high-level gymnastics with a ball. It requires balance, footwork, skill, and coordination, all at a high rate of speed. Not so simple.

And unlike gymnastics or swimming or golf, in basketball every move a player makes has the potential to be physically disrupted by another person. So practice takes on a new meaning. Basketball practice must achieve a level where players not only remember every basic move with their heads and master every move with their bodies; to truly be exceptional, players must also remember every move with their bodies. The basics of the game must become instinctual.

For young basketball players, practice is first about learning the right way, the most efficient and effective way to complete each skill. Then practice is about drilling these motor skills to rehearse the body.

The goal: *Players can respond instantaneously in any game situation, offensively or defensively, because they are no longer thinking about how to do anything.* The fundamental moves are coming as easy as breathing, and with as little thought, so the players can keep their full attention on that particular moment of that particular game. And with full confidence that the body will respond exactly as it's been trained.

If you as a coach can take young people and teach them basketball skills correctly in the beginning, these young people will have such an advantage. Ask experienced coaches and they'll all concur—an incorrect technique is very difficult to break once it becomes habit.

Take shooting, for example. Shooting is one of the hardest skills to master correctly. In high schools, there are millions of kids playing basketball, but only a very small percentage are great shooters. Even watching the more talented players in college or NBA games on TV, it's hard to find many shooters.

You can find players who can make baskets. Making a basket means a player hoists up 10 shots and maybe makes 4 of them. A shooter, however, might make 7 or 8 of those 10 shots. This shooter has practiced tens of thousands of shots, using the proper technique. And this shooter, when guarded in a game, will still make 5 or 6 of those shots. How many shots will the basket maker complete while guarded? Maybe 1 or 2. If a player can't really shoot, once you add any defense, the percentage of baskets goes way down.

This same decline is true for all the fundamental skills. Anyone can throw a pass. But only certain players can pass when they're under pressure. The players who can pass in a tight game situation are the players who have learned and drilled their skills.

And the skills work together like stones building a wall. If a player can't dribble, he can't get himself open to take a shot. If a player can shoot but can't catch, she'll rarely end up with the ball in hand to attempt the basket. Or if a player can catch but has no footwork, he can't move to position himself to take a good shot. A wall missing stones is weak, and likely to collapse.

Learned versus Innate: Which Wins?

Drilling the skills into these young bodies sounds good, but are the kids executing the best moves in a game merely those who have the most innate athletic ability?

Celtics coach John Carroll would tell you no; a player's competence in game situations is very minimally about natural ability. "One out of 100 kids may have natural ability. The other 99 have the choice of learning and drilling the proper skills. And there's not a coach on the planet that doesn't want a sound fundamental player on his team. Athletic players may shine at an earlier age, but at some point this advantage levels out, and kids with fundamental skills will go right by athletic kids that haven't learned the proper techniques."

Teach your team the correct basics and every young person on your team, regardless of natural ability, can be one of those players who can play basketball . . . one of those chosen repeatedly to get sent in and play the game they want to play.

Making Practice Fit Your Players

You've got your team, you've got your practice time, the kids are ready to go. But you're bracing for a chorus of groans and grimaces when you begin practice with drills. Maybe you're remembering how much you disliked drills as a kid. They want to play the game, your youngsters will tell you. *Coach, can't we just play?*

"It's no question that in today's society of instant gratification, what I'm suggesting, a steady diet of drills, requires a lot of diligence and discipline," Coach Carroll admits.

But don't underestimate your young team. Coach Carroll has coached multitudes of young players and, when practice is handled appropriately, has marveled at their willingness from a very young age to be in a gym working on fundamental skills.

The key to keeping the kids interested is in providing developmentally appropriate practices, designed for the size, strength, and ability level of your team. Then you can run practices that not only impart the information and the experience you want the kids to learn, but are fun, too.

"To young kids who have never played basketball, drills are not tedious. They're all brand new, so if the kids are interested in basketball, the beginning stages are novel. You introduce more as they go along so practice is not a staid activity."

For beginning players of any age, you're encouraging the kids to execute the skills correctly; slowly, but correctly, over and over and over.

Coaching more advanced players who already have some proficiency in their skills doesn't necessarily mean increasing complexity. Your nine-year-olds aren't ready for the give and go just because they've figured out the basics of the pass.

"Most of our practices with the Celtics start with some of the simplest drills," says Coach Carroll. "Two-man lay-ups, two-man lay-ups with a dribble move, two-man lay-ups with a pass. If a pro team doesn't have to do complicated drills, why would young kids have to?"

The key to drills over time is that once players have reached a level of proficiency, you as a coach get them to do everything at a higher rate of speed. "Challenge them to go harder, to go faster. Use a stopwatch. See how many they can do. You're stimulating your participants by pushing them to make them better. Get them out of their comfort zone." For at its highest level, basketball is a game of speed.

As your players become more advanced, don't be afraid to encourage them to make mistakes. Initially, they may get frustrated that they aren't able to execute the skills the way they used to. But if a child dribbles the ball off her foot, or loses his balance by pushing too much, as a teacher you know those children are extending themselves by trying to get better. Support them through this process and the kids will begin to realize they're making fewer mistakes, and they've reached a whole new level in their ability to move the ball.

Remember Your Age Group, Always

The biggest trap for coaches teaching younger kids is that they forget whom they are teaching. Scrap any cinematic fantasies of yourself holding forth to a captivated team gathered around your playboard. You will not be giving any lectures, nor will your team be sitting quietly, listening, spellbound.

- Keep your talking to a minimum when introducing a new skill. Demonstrate, then get the kids involved. You're better off stopping them a minute or two into the drill and giving them another 30 seconds of demonstration. Don't expect them to sit down and listen while you do all the talking and the moving.

- Remember that kids of a young age see humor in everything. They love to laugh, and a group is a tempting audience. You want their attention on you, not on Melissa's Band-Aid where the cartoon picture opens its mouth when she wiggles her finger. To keep their attention, you have to keep things moving.

- Expect the unexpected. Young people run through cycles of emotions and energy quickly. Your team could arrive rambunctious or run down. Maybe they woke up on a Saturday morning rarin' to go, or maybe they've come from a tiring day at school and an afternoon of homework. Be ready for the different moods and energy levels you may encounter with mutable practice plans to meet that mood.

CHAPTER 2

PRACTICE BASICS

This book's only presumption is that you, the coach, have an interest in the sport of basketball and some overall knowledge of how the game is played. You may or may not have coaching experience. But with this guide, using drills and games and age-group guidelines to customize your practice, whatever the ages of your young players, you can coach.

Each skills chapter has a section of *Drills* in order from simplest to most advanced. *Step It Up* gives suggestions for how to evolve and/or increase the difficulty of the drill. *Duration* is a suggested amount of time to allot during your practice to *run* that drill or game. The first time you introduce a skill, you will need to allot more minutes to introduce and teach the drill. The drills are followed by *Games* to play using the skill introduced in the chapter, and sometimes using a composite of skills introduced in the book.

Chapter 3 gives you an overview of the drills and games in a framework to aid you in designing practice plans for your specific group. As you begin to understand the needs of your team, you can, of course, modify the plans for your own completely custom routine. You will be able to confidently walk on the practice floor, ready to teach your team correct habits and effectively use your full practice.

EXPERIENCE TALKS: Build in a few more minutes than you think you'll need in your overall practice plan to transition from drill to drill, especially if you're working with younger children. Then select a couple of extra drills or games to have in reserve. If you end up long on time, you can fill in with one of these choices. If your practice schedule is crammed from the start, you're setting yourself up for a fall when your youngsters get off your carefully planned timeline.

Basket Height

When it comes to basket height, and ball size for that matter, Coach Carroll has some basic rules he feels strongly about—rules that may challenge the guidelines in your town, or what your area recreation department has always done. And here's the reason. Ten-foot hoops, and regulation-sized basketballs, are geared for high school, college, and professional players. This equipment is not geared for girls and boys in elementary school or even all those in middle school. When someone starts lifting weights, a trainer isn't going to start him or her with 200 pounds. Likewise, you don't want to start out your young basketball players with improperly sized equipment that makes the game tedious and too difficult. You want them to have fun. You invite them to have success by taking size and strength issues out of the equation.

Group I—Below Third Grade

"With the youngest kids, make the basket as low as you can make it. Start at 6 feet. You do not want height, size, weight, or strength to be a factor. No basket should be higher than the kids can shoot at. You want them to be able to get a handle on the ball and to shoot it with the proper technique, not hoist it or hurl it at the basket." If the baskets you're using are not adjustable, look into portable baskets or attachment baskets that fasten onto existing baskets and provide a lower target.

Group II—Third through Fifth Grade

For third graders, 6 or 7 feet can be a good height. For fourth and fifth graders, try 7 to 8 feet. But always, the height of the basket should be related to the strength and ability of the kids you're teaching. "Most kids are not shooting the ball yet at this age," says Coach Carroll. "A basket that's too high just encourages them to throw it up and not shoot properly."

Group III—Sixth Grade and Above

Your objective is to have kids shooting at a 10-foot basket by sixth or seventh grade. But remember that everything you do should be a progression. Part of teaching is reinforcing a positive thought. "You want the kids to have a feeling in their mind and a feeling in their body— they're confident that they can do this," says Coach Carroll. "When I'm teaching a new move with sixth or seventh graders, like a left-hand lay-up or left-hand hook shot, I'll lower the basket to 9 feet. It's the move that's the important part. As they become more proficient and stronger, they can begin to practice the move on a 10-foot basket."

EXPERIENCE TALKS: Consider introducing a sign that means "quiet"—perhaps a hand over your head, or a peace sign. Use the sign and stop everything until movement and noise stops. You don't want to waste your voice and valuable talking time having to say "Hold the balls" several times throughout practice.

Ball Size

Group I—Below Third Grade

With the youngest group, use a regulation women's basketball, a 28½-inch ball. Ideally, the kids each bring their own. This can be somewhat wild during practice, because most kids find it nearly impossible to hold the ball, but you want them to be actively learning as much as possible. If they have to wait for their turn with a ball, they're not only wasting learning time, they're unoccupied and free to come up with an alternate activity.

Group II—Third through Fifth Grade

For this age group, the women's ball is still appropriate. Resist the temptation to go with a men's regulation-sized ball even as your players in this age group get bigger. You want them to have plenty of time to perfect their skills without making strength or hand size an issue. The national AAU (Amateur Athletic Union) tournaments, which set the youth standard in this sport, do not use men's regulation balls until seventh grade.

Group III—Sixth Grade and Above

Now is the time to consider introducing a men's regulation-sized ball, 30 inches, to your boys' team. The girls are set; they are already using the women's regulation ball. As an added benefit, two-colored or red, white, and blue balls allow you to see the rotation on the ball during shooting drills and can be an aid in coaching the proper shooting technique.

Number of Coaches and Players

The easiest practice number to work with is 10 kids. This divides easily into two groups of five for drills, and the most playing time in a game. Many coaches like to have 12 players on the team, so having 10 kids present at any given practice becomes more of a surety. You can also practice with eight and divide into four on four. Or pair the kids up and have them work with each other, matching those who are progressing more quickly together, and those working on a more rudimentary level together. So ideally, the number of players on your team is 8 to 12. More than 10 to 12 kids to work with and a single coach is going to find it hard to keep everyone's attention.

If you choose to have more players on your team—you're going to be working consistently with 10 to 15 players—look for an assistant. This assistant is not some NCAA champ who wants to talk about everything he or she knows. Age doesn't matter and gender doesn't matter. What's more important, especially with younger children, is having patience and the willingness to learn and teach. You as coaches are helping young people with their growth and learning. For many of them, their experience with you will decide whether they find the game of basketball enjoyable and want to continue playing.

Practice Expectations

Group I—Below Third Grade

In this group, you're trying to get kids to understand the fundamentals of the game. Concentrate on teaching them how to dribble, pass, and shoot.

Also make them aware that they have a big area to work with; they don't have to be all bunched together. An average practice for this age would be an hour: 45 minutes for skills, and 15 minutes for scrimmage games.

> **EXPERIENCE TALKS:** When it comes to coaching, you can throw gender considerations out the window. If you have (for instance) a first-grade team that's mostly boys, and you have dads who want to be involved and have played the sport, you may not even consider enlisting a mom who's never coached or played on a team herself. But in the Carroll family, as little as Mom knew about basketball fundamentals, she actually had more to offer this age group than many of the dads, because she paid a lot more attention to what it took to keep six- and seven-year-olds engaged and interested. The basketball techniques that a coach might cover with a group this young can be learned in a short amount of time (which she did); having long-term experience with young kids is much more valuable.

Group II—Third through Fifth Grade

Young kids instinctively go after the ball like a swarm of bees to honey. Now is when to break this habit. Begin to work concretely with the concept of spacing, of each player creating room to operate. Here you're teaching advanced levels of passing, catching, dribbling, and shooting, and concentrating on using the entire playing area. You can begin developing the concepts of defense with man-to-man drills. An average practice for this age would be 1 1/4 to 1 1/2 hours: 55 to 70 minutes for skills, and 20 minutes for free-throw practice and a scrimmage game.

Group III—Sixth Grade and Above

Start integrating the fundamental skills into the team concepts of offense and defense. Coach your players to make offensive and defensive moves with more precision, and work now on a regular basis with the concept of five on five. Young people at this age can be expected to come to practice prepared to play, and to accomplish something individually and as a team. An average practice for this age would be 1½ to 2 hours: 70 to 95 minutes for skills, and 20 to 25 minutes for free-throw practice and a scrimmage game.

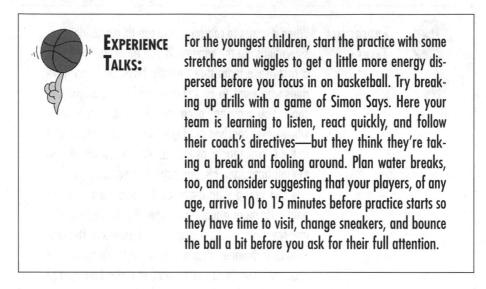

EXPERIENCE TALKS: For the youngest children, start the practice with some stretches and wiggles to get a little more energy dispersed before you focus in on basketball. Try breaking up drills with a game of Simon Says. Here your team is learning to listen, react quickly, and follow their coach's directives—but they think they're taking a break and fooling around. Plan water breaks, too, and consider suggesting that your players, of any age, arrive 10 to 15 minutes before practice starts so they have time to visit, change sneakers, and bounce the ball a bit before you ask for their full attention.

Equipment

Other than a basketball court, the players need shoes appropriate for the court, and ideally they will all have a ball the correct size for their age. In addition, useful tools for you, the coach, include a whistle and small orange cones (or markers, which are shorter and less expensive); these can be purchased in most sporting goods stores. A few of the games call for colored pinneys to differentiate teams. To diagram positions or drills, purchase a playboard and dry marker set to use or make your own court template.

The Court

The *baseline* or *end line* is the line at each end of the court (found behind the basket) that delineates the court; the *sideline* is either line siding the court. Inside these lines, or on the court, is *in-bounds;* outside these lines, or off the court, is *out-of-bounds.* The *foul line* is the line that borders the high end of the painted area. This painted rectangle on the court below the basket is called the *paint;* it is also referred to as the *lane* or *key. Box* refers to the boxes marked on the foul lane; there are two, one on either side of the basket. *Elbow* refers to the corner where the foul line and painted lane meet; there are two. The ***top of the key*** is the high point of the circle marked at the end of the paint farthest away from the basket. *Center circle* is the court's center circle.

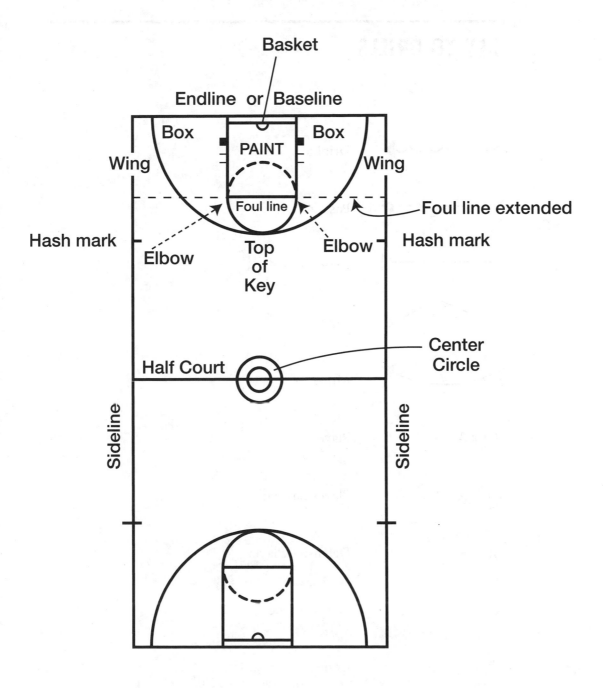

KEY TO DRILLS

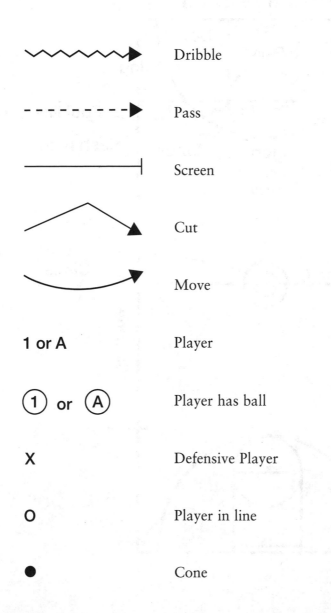

∿∿∿▶	Dribble
- - - -▶	Pass
⊢	Screen
▲	Cut
⌒▶	Move
1 or A	Player
① or Ⓐ	Player has ball
X	Defensive Player
O	Player in line
●	Cone

CHAPTER 3

DESIGNING YOUR PRACTICE

Preparing a practice plan is similar to writing a term paper. But unlike some term papers, practice can be a fun activity, for you and the kids.

First, make yourself some notes (the outline) about what you want to do, what you want to achieve, how much time you have. Next, write up a sample practice plan (the rough draft) and tinker with it. Then rewrite your final version.

After practice, make yourself some more notes. Evaluate how the different drills and games were handled by your group, what was too difficult, your team's weak areas, ideas for the next practice. The more time you spend on your plans outside of practice, the more organized and relaxed you will be during practice.

Running practice, however, is not an exact science, but more of an art. Every group is going to be slightly different, and you want to be gauging your practices for your group. For younger kids, the practice plan is not as critical. You're going to be introducing a lot of new things, alternating drills with games to keep them enjoying learning this game of basketball.

For all age groups, remind yourself often that at times you will just have to move on, even if your players haven't begun to master what you're teaching. They will learn over time, and with repetition. Just keep your descriptions as short and quick as possible, and keep the kids involved by asking them questions to see if they know what you're talking about, and getting them up and involved demonstrating or trying out the skill or technique as soon as possible.

The charts and practice plans that follow are designed to start you out with a sample outline and rough draft. You can then tinker with these as you get to know your players and begin to feel comfortable customizing for their needs.

If you are coaching a team in the Group II bracket, be sensitive to the fact that some of the drills mentioned here are going to be too complex for inexperienced third graders; and may be too complex for fourth or fifth graders if you have a lot of kids who have not played organized basketball before. In each chapter, the drills are generally presented in order from simplest to most complex, so if you know your kids are low on experience for their age, start in with the lower-number drills until you gauge their ability. On the other hand, if you have a team of fundamentally strong fifth graders who have been playing together since first grade, you may consider trying a few Group III drills before your season is finished. Or for Group III, as the season goes on, you may decide you really need to spend one practice doing 30 minutes of offensive moves, or maybe 45 minutes on different aspects of playing defense. So do it. You're the coach, and if they've been adequately prepared, this age group can handle a more specific focus.

Just remember, again, basketball is a game. Your job as a coach is to enhance the enjoyment of the game.

Confident Coach's Drill Guide

Skills	Age Groups		
	GROUP I	GROUP II	GROUP III
Ball handling	Drills 1–4	All drills	All drills
Dribbling	Drills 1–4	All drills	All drills
	Game 1	All games	All games
Passing	Drills 1–5	Drills 1–7	All drills
	Game 1	All games	All games
Shooting	Drills 1–5	Drills 1–16	All drills
	Games 1–2	All games	All games
Defense			
Transition	Drill 1	All drills	All drills
Individual	Drills 1–3	All drills	All drills
Team	———	Drill 1	All drills
	Game 1	All games	All games

Skills	Age Groups		
	GROUP I	**GROUP II**	**GROUP III**
Offense	Drill 1	Drills 2–6	Drills 2–9
Jab series	Drill 1	Drills 1–3	All drills
	Game 1	All games	All games
Rebounding	Drills 1–3	Drills 1–9	All drills
	Game 1	All games	All games
Agility	Drills 1–5	All drills	All drills
	All games	All games	Game 2

Group I Sample Practice

1 hour practice: 45 minutes skills/15 minutes scrimmage game

5 minutes	Agility and warm-up
5–10 minutes	Ball handling*
10 minutes	Dribbling*
10 minutes	Passing*
5 minutes	Rebounding*
10 minutes	Shooting

*Include three of these four sections per practice, alternating between games and drills for the skills work. With more advanced players in this group, you could keep two of these four sections and add an offense or defense selection.

Group II Sample Practice

1¼–1½ hour practice: 55–70 minutes skills/20 minutes free throws and scrimmage

5 minutes	Agility and warm-up
5 minutes	Ball handling*
10 minutes	Dribbling*
5 minutes	Passing*
10 minutes	Shooting
10–15 minutes	Defense
5 minutes	Rebounding
10–15 minutes	Offense

*Choose two of these three sections to include per practice.

Group III Sample Practice

1¾–2 hour practice: 85–100 minutes skills/20–25 minutes free throws and scrimmage

5 minutes	Agility and warm-up
10 minutes	Ball handling
10 minutes	Dribbling
10 minutes	Passing
15 minutes	Shooting
15–20 minutes	Defense
5–10 minutes	Rebounding
15–20 minutes	Offense

EXPERIENCE TALKS:

There is a reason we keep harping on having fun. We've sat through practices where we've watched coaches—good people and good parents—get lost in bad scenarios. For example, practicing a complicated weave drill with eight- and nine-year-olds who, amazingly enough, didn't catch on. The dad kept at it, with growing frustration, for a very long time, finishing in a bad mood, having snapped at his own sons, with none of the team much closer to understanding what he was talking about, but quite sure they didn't want to do any kind of weave in the near or distant future.

And we've sat through some games that were extremely hard to watch. For example, an assistant coaching staff (for a third-grade team), made up of two fathers over and above the two who were coaching, sat on the bench with computer spreadsheet packets, keeping enough statistics on each player to rival the sports section of any major city paper. The "staff" then used these statistics to talk to the players after the game about areas where they just weren't coming up with the numbers, or where their opponents were.

EXPERIENCE TALKS:

continued...

Now, if this is you, or any of the parents you've coached with, have a sense of humor, chuckle a bit, and start fresh. Coaching youth basketball is not about how much you know—as with our offensive guru; nor is it about breaking down the kids' spirit and the excitement of the game—as was happening with our rambunctious numbers-crunching "staff." Teach your players fundamentals and you've done your job. The best coaches simply instill a little bit of structure within which kids can play the game they love to play.

Part II

ESSENTIAL SKILLS

CHAPTER 4

THE ART OF BALL HANDLING AND DRIBBLING

Ball Handling

What is the purpose of doing ball-handling drills? A player doesn't actually use these techniques in a game. *Why do we have to do these, Coach?*

"Sometimes these drills do seem to be done just to impress people," says Coach Carroll. "When I was growing up, I remember teams coming out before high school and college games doing these drills and getting the crowd revved up. It was more of a showcase performance than anything. But the true point of ball handling is to develop a feel for the ball and a confidence in handling the ball. Many people would say, ultimately, a basketball player wants to feel like the ball is an extension of his or her hand."

Following are 10 warm-up drills that a coach can teach in practice, and that players can do almost anywhere. Do each drill for 60 seconds. For many of them, all a player needs is a ball; for the rest, a ball and a small area of flat surface. You as a coach can encourage your players to prepare for practice with a warm-up series. It will prepare them much more effectively for walking onto the court than a current popular method—picking up a ball and taking a three-point shot that they're not tall enough or strong enough to take in the first place, even warmed up.

Drills

1. SLAP THE BALL

Hold the ball in front and just slap it hard, back and forth, from hand to hand. This causes blood to rush to the fingers, sensitizing them, and getting the hands warmed up.

2. FINGERTIPS

With arms straight overhead, tap the ball back and forth between the fingertips, keeping the ball alive. With arms still outstretched and tapping the ball back and forth, slowly move the arms down in front of the face, the chest, and continue down to the knees, then slowly reverse to finish back up over the head.

3. AROUND THE WORLD

Standing with legs together, knees bent to start, take the ball and pass it around the legs, then around the hips, around the waist/chest, around the head, and back down again. Do the same series changing direction and going the opposite way around the body.

4. AROUND THE LEGS

With the legs spread apart, bending over, pass the ball around one leg; then jump with the legs together and pass the ball around both legs; then jump with the legs apart and pass the ball around the other leg; then put the legs back together, and so on, back and forth.

5. FIGURE EIGHT

With the legs apart and the body bent forward at the waist, pass the ball around one leg, then the other, then back, to make a continual figure eight, keeping the head up; then switch direction and make the figure eight the opposite way.

6. AROUND-THE-LEG DRIBBLE

In an athletic or defensive position, knees bent, down low with a ball, dribble completely around the right leg using only the right hand for

30 seconds; then go around the left leg using only the left hand for 30 seconds.

7. FIGURE-EIGHT DRIBBLE

This drill expands on the around-the-leg dribble. This time dribble once and around the right leg with the right hand, then bounce-pass to the left hand and dribble the ball once around the left leg, back and forth, to form a figure eight. After 30 seconds, reverse direction.

8. TAKE A BREAK

Sit down flat on the floor or ground, legs open in a V in front. Dribble between the legs alternating hands after each dribble, first right, then left; then move to dribble on the left side with the left hand; then go back to the center to continue as started; then move to dribble on the right side with the right hand. The face is forward; the eyes are not on the ball.

9. UNDER THE BRIDGE

With the legs in a side straddle, slam the ball down to bounce between the legs under the body, then catch the ball behind the back as it comes back up. Bring the ball around front and do again.

10. FERRIS WHEEL

With the legs again in side straddle, slam the ball down between the legs and catch in back, then throw it from the back to arc over the head and catch in front. (The goal here is to be able to do this while standing in basically the same spot.)

Dribbling

Dribbling is a very important part of basketball, like passing, because it advances the ball. It is also an abused skill. Or perhaps *overused* would be a more accurate description, for one critical reason: *Passing advances the ball much quicker than dribbling.* You can demonstrate this physically to your players by having them move the ball down the court using the two methods side by side.

That said, dribbling does have a purpose. Indeed, dribbling should always have a purpose. Therefore, a player wants to learn when to dribble and when not to dribble.

A player should use the dribble to:

- Move the ball up for fast-break basketball.
- Advance the ball against the pressure of full-court defense.
- Penetrate and create plays.
- Change angles to create better passing.

A player should not use a dribble to:

- Stand in place.
- Go sideways for no reason.
- Go into a congested area of players.

First off, as a coach, you want to avoid the common tendency of teaching your kids to catch the ball and start bouncing. A player should generally catch the ball in triple-threat position and survey all the options first. Once players catch the ball and dribble once or twice, their options are gone. Their full vision is gone, their quickest option to pass or shoot is gone, and their best opportunity at getting by the defense before the other team is in place is gone.

Your players do want to learn to dribble effectively with both hands and to keep their head up, not down looking at the dribble.

These are the different techniques used in dribbling that you want your players to master. The ultimate goal is the ability to execute all these moves at a high rate of speed without taking anything from their ability to see the court.

- **Control dribble.** This is a basic dribble, used when closely guarded by the opposition and the ball needs to be protected. The player is in an athletic stance, knees bent, head up, the nondribbling arm bent at the elbow and held up around waist height to protect the ball. The ball hand is in a relaxed position, fingers slightly flexed and spread across the ball. The force comes from flexing the wrist and pushing the ball down to the floor hard using the pads of the fingers. The ball is not dribbled off the palm of the hand. In a control dribble, the ball should not bounce any higher than about knee height

Control dribble.

-  **Speed dribble.** This is for moving the ball down the court quickly when not closely guarded. For this dribble, the player is running, pushing the ball out in front, and allowing the ball to come up to about waist height.

Speed dribble.

- **Stutter step.** This puts a defender off balance. From a speed dribble, the player comes to a jump stop, then stutter-steps, taking little steps in place back and forth sideways so the defender doesn't know which way the player is going to go, until she busts out into a speed dribble again, and is gone.

- **Hesitation.** This causes a defender to relax for an instant. From a speed dribble, slow to a near stop to take the defender off guard, then push out again in a speed dribble.

- **Backup.** When an offensive player is being pressured, this move creates enough space to maneuver and to obtain better vision of the court. From a speed dribble, come to a jump stop balanced on both feet, shoulder width apart, knees slightly bent. Then, more slowly, step back and slide the front foot to follow, then step back and slide again to complete two slides backward.

Crossover. This allows a player to change direction. From a speed dribble, come up to the defender, then, as low as possible, push the ball from the right hand to the left or left hand to the right, and then shoot by the player in a different direction with the ball now in the other hand. (This is a difficult move; it takes a lot of practice for a player to be able to pick up the ball quickly with the new hand and continue the dribble without missing a beat.)

Crossover (left).

Behind the back (right).

Inside out. This is the companion move to the crossover. Begin a crossover move, but just before sending the ball to the other hand, cup the ball hand and turn the wrist to bring the ball back to the same side. Then head off in that direction.

Between the legs. Another way to change direction, this dribble is useful because the ball is not exposed in front of the player. This move is similar to a crossover, but instead of the ball crossing from one hand to the other in front of the body, the ball is bounced through the player's legs as the player steps forward.

Behind the back. This is an advanced move to confuse the defender. The player speed-dribbles right at the defender, who will think the player's going to continue—but instead the player cups his hand and pulls his arm back behind himself to push the ball down hard behind his back. The ball bounces up from behind his back into his opposite hand.

> **EXPERIENCE TALKS:** The key to changing speed and direction is the player's ability to go by the defender as closely as possible. To get by a defender, the player goes low, and tight to the defender's shoulder, then explodes by before the defender can move. If the player is too far away from the defender, the defender has time and room to move and get in the way. Give your players the concept of moving north–south in a straight line to the basket, not east–west to the sides.

Drills

1. POUND THE BALL

Each player has a ball, and all are spaced out on the court. The drill begins with each player in a control-dribble position, pounding the ball down to the floor in a hard dribble with the right hand for 60 seconds, then pounding the ball with the left hand. Do the series two or three times.

DURATION: 4–6 minutes.

2. SIR DRIBBLE

Each player gets down on one knee. The drill is to pound the ball with the right hand on the right side, then hard crossover-dribble under the knee to the left hand to continue with pounding the ball on the left side, and then hard crossover-dribble under the knee back to the right side. Do one side for 60 to 90 seconds, then switch knees and do the series again.

DURATION: 2–3 minutes.

3. DRIBBLE LINES

Divide the team in half and line the players up on opposite sidelines, spread from baseline to baseline. The two lines will dribble toward each other across the court, with each player finishing by going to the end of the opposing group's line. The drill starts with the player at the front of each line doing a right-hand dribble to the other side of the court. Go through the whole line, and then switch to the next move in the series. This series can run as follows:

Dribble lines, crossing at the cone.

◎   Dribble with the right hand.

◎   Dribble with the left hand.

◎   Dribble to the center until even with the other player, hesitate by slowing the pace, then continue to other sideline.

◎   Dribble to the center, stutter, then continue.

◎   Dribble to the center, cross over and go around the player coming from the other direction, then continue.

◎   Dribble to the center, stutter, then cross over, go around the player, and continue.

◎   Dribble to the center, then inside out, go around the player, and continue.

- ⊕ Dribble to the center, then between the legs while passing the other player, and continue.
- ⊕ Dribble to the center, then behind the back while passing the other player, and continue.

DURATION: 8–10 minutes.

4. CONTROL DRIBBLE

Line up pairs of kids along the baseline, one behind the other. The first person in line has a ball, and dribbles out to the foul line or foul line extended. This player then pivots to face her partner and goes into a control dribble—athletic position, knees bent, body low, nondribbling arm up to protect the ball, dribbling hard with the ball coming no higher than the knee. The player does this with her right hand for 15 seconds, then crosses over to control-dribble with her left hand for 15 seconds, then dribbles back to her partner; the partner then does the series. Each player can do the series two to three times.

STEP IT UP: The person at the baseline holds up one, two, or three fingers, and the person dribbling has to keep calling out how many fingers are held up. This forces the dribbler to keep her head up, as it should be, and not down watching the ball.

DURATION: 3–5 minutes.

5. HARD CROSSOVERS

Players each have a ball and dribble as hard as they can while continually crossing over in front of the body, left to right to left to right.

STEP IT UP: Evolve the pattern to two hard dribbles with the right hand, then crossover-dribble to the left hand; two hard dribbles with the left hand, then crossover-dribble to the right; and so on.

DURATION: 2–3 minutes.

6. BACKDOOR FIGURE EIGHT

The drill is a figure eight going through the legs from the back. The player takes one to three dribbles with the right hand to go around the right leg, then bounce-passes the ball to the left hand and continues with one to three dribbles around the left leg to bounce-pass it from behind to the right hand, and so on.

DURATION: 2–3 minutes.

7. FOLLOW THE LEADER

The team follows the first person in line in a tour around the court on the baseline, following the moves of the leader as the leader dribbles with the right hand, with the left hand, crosses over, behind the back, through the legs.

DURATION: 3–5 minutes.

8. DRIBBLE MOVES

Divide the team into two lines on each side of the center circle, A on the right, B on the left. Each player in line A has a ball. Set up one cone at the right elbow. The first player in line A dribbles at the cone with his

Dribble moves, attacking the cone.

right hand, then around it to the basket to make a lay-up, while the first person in line B comes down on the other side and gets the rebound. Each player returns to the end of the opposite line, as the next people in line start the drill.

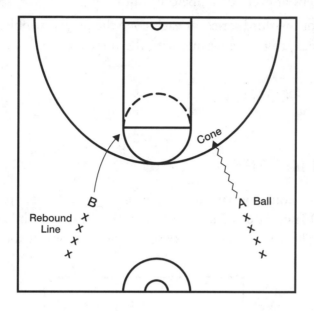

Proceed in a series with the right hand as follows: stutter; crossover; stutter-crossover; inside out; between the legs; behind the back. Then move the cone to the left elbow, and have players do the series with their left hand.

STEP IT UP: Put the cones in different places and make the shot a jump shot.

DURATION: 10–15 minutes.

9. ZIGZAG DRIBBLE

Seven cones are set up along the side of the court, or 14 covering both sides of the court, as diagrammed. The team lines up at the beginning corner.

A. The first person dribbles to the first cone with the right hand; crosses over at the cone and continues with the left hand; crosses over at the cone and continues with the right hand; and so on. The next player in line can start when the preceding player reaches the first cone.

B. For the second series, instead of just a crossover at the cone, each player does a crossover, then retreats, backing up two steps at every cone, before continuing.

C. For the third series, at each cone the player dribbles behind the back, to then continue with the opposite hand.

DURATION: 5–10 minutes.

10. BEAT THE CONE

Line up five cones down the middle of the court. Group 1 can walk while dribbling; groups 2 and 3 want to go full speed while dribbling at the cone. The series is as follows, making the move at the cone to get

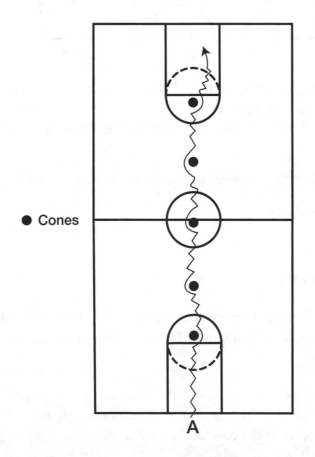

● Cones

A

around the cone as if getting around a defensive player: crossover; inside out; between the legs; stutter; stutter-crossover; behind the back.

DURATION: 5 minutes.

11. CIRCLE DRIBBLE

Put four or five cones in a random pattern in the center and/or jump circles. If you have enough cones, you can have three groups going at the same time. The first player dribbles around the cones in any configuration with her right hand for 15 to 30 seconds. You can blow the whistle or yell "Change," and the next player does the same thing, et cetera. For the second series, have players dribble with their left hand.

DURATION: 3–5 minutes.

Games

1. DRIBBLE TAG

This is a game of tag, but every player has a ball and has to dribble to move. Set boundaries for the playing area; the younger the children, the smaller the space. The person who is It tags with the nondribbling hand, and then that new person is It. A variation would be to also make any player who loses the ball out-of-bounds automatically It.

DURATION: 5 minutes.

2. POKE

To teach this to young children, you can start with two kids in the court center circle as a boundary, or you can use the paint as a boundary and start with three kids. Each player has a ball and has to dribble to move. The object of the game is to poke the other players' balls away. To play with a whole team of 10 to 12 players, use the half court as the area. For more than 12 older players, have them spread out over the full court. Once a player's ball is poked away, that player is out. The winner is the last person left with a ball.

DURATION: 5–10 minutes.

3. HALF-COURT HUSTLE

This is a popular Celtics halftime game with audience contestants. To set up, two balls are placed in the middle of the center circle, one on either side of the half-court line. The first two players are on the sideline at the half-court line. When the coach starts them with "On your mark, get set, go," they run to the center, grab the ball on their side of the court, and run, dribbling, to their basket to make a lay-up. If they miss, they shoot until they get a basket. Then they run, dribbling, back to the center circle. The first one there wins; the other player is eliminated. Then the next pair plays, and so forth, until everyone has taken a turn. Then the winners from the elimination round play each other, and the pair-offs continue until one person is left as the winner.

DURATION: 8–10 minutes.

CHAPTER 5

THE ART OF PASSING

In the team game of basketball, passing is the most efficient way to move the basketball. Yet passing is one of the most overlooked and underappreciated skills in the game. The ability of the five players on the court to move the basketball with the pass is an art form. A lot of emphasis is placed on dribbling, jumping, and shooting, but a player's ability to pass the basketball is one that coaches at any level value. John Stockton, point guard for the Utah Jazz, was one of the smaller, less athletic players in basketball, but when he retired, he held the all-time record for NBA assists. The fact that he was still a starter for his team at 41 years old was strongly related to his exceptional passing ability.

There are two aspects to good passing. The first is the ability to physically send the ball to another location. The second is the ability to intuitively know when, where, and how fast to direct the pass so a designated teammate can catch it. If players haven't mastered the first aspect, they will never truly achieve the second.

The coach has the most influence in the first aspect, drilling for physical mastery of the pass. After this, the more that team members pass to each other, the more they become familiar with where their teammates are going to be, and the more their intuitive sense of finding each other improves. The drills help players master the physical ability; interaction and experience with their teammates help them master the innate sense of landing the pass.

The complement to passing that is extremely important yet isn't often talked about is catching. When you're teaching passing, you also want to be teaching catching. In the passing drills, make sure your players are focusing on the catch. The receiving player has his feet shoulder width apart, knees loose, hands up ready to catch the ball. The player's mental and visual focus is on the ball as he "watches" the ball right into his hands.

1. Chest Pass

Anytime a drill or game calls for a pass, with no other designation, this is it.

Both hands are on the ball; the stance is balanced with legs shoulder width apart, elbows tucked. All in one motion, step forward toward the destination on either foot while pushing the ball away with both hands. The wrists snap forward and the hands and arms follow through in the direction of the ball—not down toward the floor. Players can do this against a wall.

To also practice catching, divide your players in half and make this a two-line passing drill, passing to each other. Go down each line and check that each child is passing correctly.

Following through on a chest pass.

Step It Up: See if the kids can go up and down the line without dropping the ball, or count how many passes are caught consecutively.

Duration: 3–5 minutes.

2. BOUNCE PASS

This pass is used to get the ball low, below the defense's hands. It is also softer than the chest pass coming up into a teammate's hands.

With the player's body set up the same as the chest pass, push the ball to bounce on the floor two-thirds of the way to the destination. The wrists snap forward and the hands and arms follow through in the direction of the ball, this time down toward the floor.

STEP IT UP: As above, see how many catches in a row your team can achieve.

DURATION: 3–5 minutes.

3. TANDEM CHEST PASS

Divide the team in half and form two lines at the baseline. For younger players, the lines may start at about 8 feet apart; for older players, work up to 15 feet apart. The first two kids begin running the length of the court, passing the ball to each other.

STEP IT UP: Make this drill more difficult by increasing the distance between the lines.

DURATION: 3–5 minutes.

4. TANDEM BOUNCE PASS

This is similar to the previous drill, only players must use a bounce now as they run the length of the court. This is more difficult because players must begin to visualize where to aim the bounce, judging their partner's speed.

STEP IT UP: Increase the distance between the lines.

DURATION: 3–5 minutes.

5. LINE PASSING

Divide your team into two groups, one group at each basket. One player, the passer, is standing roughly at the top of the key; the other four to five players are in a line on the foul line, with the end players a few steps forward so that the line curves around the passer. Adjust the distance for the age and ability of your group. The passer has the ball, and chest-passes it to the first player at one end. That player passes it back to the passer, who then passes it to the next player, who passes it back. The drill continues to the end of the line and back. Then rotate the passer to the front end of the line; the player on the opposite end rotates up to take passer's position, and this new passer does the series. After the whole line has rotated through, the drill can be done again, this time using a bounce pass.

> **DURATION:** 3 minutes.

6. RAPID-FIRE PASSING

Divide your team into two groups, one at each basket, and set up with a passer at the top of the key; the other four to five players are in a line on the foul line, with the end players a few steps forward so that the line curves around the passer. The passer has a ball, but for this drill one of the players in line has a second ball—we'll say player 3. The passer starts by passing her ball to, for instance, player 1. Then player 3 passes her ball to the passer. The passer immediately passes this ball to, for instance, player 4, and then receives the other ball on a pass back from player 1. The drill continues with the two balls going back and forth from the central passer for 20 to 30 seconds. Then rotate the line, continuing until every player has a chance to be the central passer.

> **DURATION:** 3–5 minutes.

 **EXPERIENCE TALKS:** For younger children, the best balls to use to teach the chest and bounce pass are the mini basketballs, around 13½ inches, sold at sports stores and college and pro gift shops.

7. THREE-LINE PASSING

This is a variation on tandem passing. Players form three lines on the baseline, as far apart from each other as they can comfortably pass. Line A is the middle; lines B and C are on either side. The first players from all three lines begin running down the court. Player A passes to where B is going to be; B passes back to where A is going to be. Then A passes to where C is going to be and C passes back to where A is going to be. The sequence continues to the other end, where they turn around and come back, then giving the ball to the next three so they can start the same sequence. This drill can be repeated with bounce passes, and the position of the lines can be changed to give different players the opportunity to play the middle.

Set-up for three-line passing.

STEP IT UP: This drill can be done with two balls: After player A releases the ball to B, A swivels back to catch a pass from C. Another addition is to include a lay-up by the outside player who ends up at the baseline with the ball.

DURATION: 5–8 minutes.

8. SQUARE PASSING

With one player at each corner, A, B, C, and D, form a square with sides the length of whatever distance your players can comfortably pass—a range of somewhere between 5 and 15 feet. The remaining teammates are in line behind each of the corners. Player A passes the ball to player B. Then A jogs to B and goes to the end of the line at B, while B throws to C. B jogs to the end of the line at C while C throws to D; the pattern continues around the square. Repeat with bounce passes.

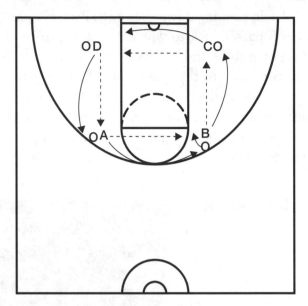

STEP IT UP: Make this drill more difficult by calling for players to increase their speed; calling for change of direction; or using one or two more balls, so players now have three balls moving around the square.

DURATION: 5–8 minutes.

9. STAR PASSING

Set up the players at the tips of a five-pointed star, with second (and third, if necessary) players lined up behind the player at each point. The diagonals should be whatever passing distance is appropriate for the age of your players. The player with the ball chest-passes to the person on the diagonal that would be the next point of the star, then goes behind the second player at the point so that player is up next for the pass. The ball movement continues to make a star. Next, do the same star pattern with a bounce pass.

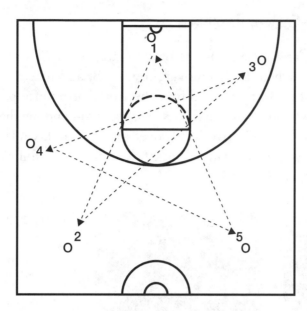

STEP IT UP: You can call for speed; count the consecutive catches; or call for a change of direction.

DURATION: 3–5 minutes.

10. SQUARE PASSING WITH HANDOFF

Set up as in square passing, Drill 8. Player A passes to B and then starts jogging toward B. Player B passes back to A—a shorter pass, because A is now closer to B. Player A catches the pass and then hands off the ball to B as he reaches the B corner, and goes to the end of the line. B then passes to C, and the pattern continues around the square.

STEP IT UP: To increase difficulty, use a bounce pass; push for speed; call for a change of direction; or add another ball.

DURATION: 5–8 minutes.

11. Four-Corner Passing

The players are at four corners of a square, A, B, C, and D. Player A starts with the ball, begins moving toward B, and passes the ball to B. For this first pass, in addition to a chest pass or bounce pass, Player A can use a two-hand overhead pass. For the two-hand overhead pass, the player takes the ball in two hands over the head and, while stepping toward the target, passes with a quick flex of the wrist, following through in the direction of the ball.

Two-hand overhead pass.

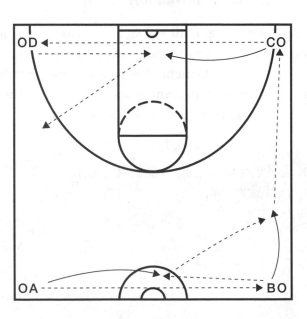

Player B immediately passes it back to A and begins moving toward C. Player A passes it to B and goes to the end of any line at the B corner. B now passes it to C, who immediately passes it back to B. Player C begins to move toward D. B passes it to C, goes to the end of any line at the C corner, and the sequence continues around the square.

STEP IT UP: Add another ball.

DURATION: 5–8 minutes.

12. PRESSURE PASSING

Two additional passes are needed for the following drill: the hook pass and the two-hand over-the-head pass.

For the hook pass, or one-hand shoulder pass, with knees loose, a player fakes low or high with the ball in two hands, extending one leg out around the body of the person defending him. At the last moment, he takes his far hand off, keeping the same side hand on the ball as the stepping leg. Forming a hook with his hand and arm, he throws a one-arm pass around the defender.

Hook pass.

For the drill, player 1 is a couple of steps above the key, with player 2 at the foul line playing defense. Player 3 is on the right box; 4 is on the left box. Player 1 dribbles at 2 and then jump-stops by jumping on both

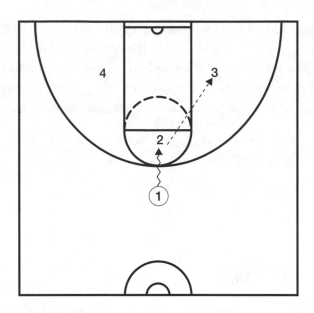

feet at the same time, shoulder width apart, evenly balanced. Pivoting on one foot (the same foot throughout), 1 turns toward 3, then toward 4, back and forth. When the coach blows the whistle, 1 puts a chest pass, bounce pass, or hook pass into the hands of 3 or 4—whichever player he's facing at the whistle. Players 3 and 4 are both crouched with hands up, ready to make a power lay-up right into the basket. After the lay-up is shot, the players can do it again from the same positions, reset by rotating among the four, or rotate a new player in and one out.

STEP IT UP: To make this drill more difficult, add a player on defense. Player 1 has the ball; 2 and 3 are attempting to block the pass; 4 and 5 are waiting on the boxes to make the lay-up. To take it up one more notch, as soon 4 is passed the ball, 5 runs over and attempts to block the shot, or vice versa.

DURATION: 5–8 minutes.

EXPERIENCE TALKS: Until a young person has a large enough hand to handle the ball, the hook pass will be difficult, and until a young person has a sufficient amount of strength, the over-the-head pass will be ineffective. Coach Carroll generally doesn't work on these passes until players are nearing or in sixth grade.

Games

1. ULTIMATE PASSING

This is a game similar to Ultimate Frisbee, only with a basketball. Divide your group into two recognizable teams using colored pinneys or some other method to differentiate the team members. No dribbling is allowed. The goal is to make completed passes to teammates. The game can be played to 6 points; to 12 points; or whatever you decide.

A. **Beginning Ultimate Passing.** The team that's on offense and starting with the ball has four players; the team on defense has three. All players must stay in-bounds using half the court. One point is earned when the team on offense completes four consecutive passes. If the pass is intercepted, one of the four rotates out, and the team that had three players rotates a player in so they have four. The new team on offense now attempts to complete as many sequences of four passes as they can before the other team intercepts the ball. Team members on the side can substitute in as the ball changes hands, or two games can be going on, using the two half courts.

B. **Ultimate Passing.** The game is the same, only team members are of equal numbers on each side, making the players work harder to get open, as they would in a game. With four or six kids in the game, use a half court and teams of two or three. With older kids, you could play the game with four-plus players on each team using the full court.

C. **Advanced Ultimate Passing.** Create your own variations depending upon the skill level of your team. One variation is to give two points for a basket (but still no dribbling allowed). Within this game, a team may get a bonus point for five consecutive passes, or for any bounce passes.

DURATION: 8–10 minutes.

2. MONKEY IN THE MIDDLE

This game is better with older players, because of the need for hook and two-hand overhead passes. Line up in groups of three, with one player in the middle. Using mostly two-hand overhead or hook passes, the two on the outside pass to each other. The person in the middle—the "monkey"—is on defense and can do anything she wants to touch, deflect, or stop the ball. When the monkey gets her hands on the ball, the person who threw that pass goes into the middle and the monkey takes that position on the outside. The two main rules are that the person in the middle cannot go any closer than an arm's length to the two outside people, and the two outside people cannot throw high lob passes.

DURATION: 5–8 minutes.

CHAPTER 6

THE ART OF SHOOTING

Shooting is the most important skill in the game of basketball. The reason is obvious: The ultimate goal of the game is to put the ball in the basket. If players can shoot, they can play this game. If players can't shoot, they become a liability to the team, even if all their other skills are honed to a high level. Great shooting makes up for a multitude of weaknesses.

"Shooting is a tremendous weapon," says Coach Carroll. "It opens up your whole game. When you can shoot, your defender has to play you tight. When the defender is in close, it increases your opportunities to drive by and score. And not only does your game open up, this opens up the game for your teammates. Your shooting ability dictates how you will be played when you have the ball, and when you don't."

It's an absolute fallacy that great shooters are born, says Coach Carroll. "People talk about natural shooters, because great shooters make it look so easy. But in reality, great shooters are made, not born," insists this almost 30-year coaching veteran. "Great shooters have practiced hundreds of thousands of shots for hours and hours and hours, in the gym, the court, the backyard. All it takes is a player, a ball, and a hoop. I'm convinced that if young people were given the fundamentals of shooting and instilled with a work ethic to learn to shoot, there would be a lot more great shooters. And the great thing about shooting is that it's like bike riding: It's a skill you never lose."

But as with a bicycle, start with training wheels first.

The key to young athletes becoming shooters is learning the fundamentals correctly, then continuing through progressions of difficulty, with repetition at every stage, for all ages. To begin shooting, players stand still right at the basket and shoot. Then they move back from the basket, stand still, and shoot. Then farther back, stand still, and shoot. Next, they work on increasing the speed with which they can get the ball off their hands correctly and into the basket. Then they add movement before the shot and practice shooting off a dribble. Lastly, they practice completing all these skills while being guarded, as in a game situation.

Mental Confidence

Nowhere in the game of basketball is mental confidence as important as it is in shooting. Technical proficiency being equal, mental confidence is what makes a great shooter out of a good one. Make sure your players are shooting at appropriate-height baskets with balls they can wield. You want your young players to have confidence about their ability to shoot from the very beginning. One of the quickest ways to destroy young people's confidence in their ability to get that ball in the basket is to have them in front of baskets that are too high, or using balls that are too big.

You as a coach can also instill mental strength by stressing to your players that the more they practice—repeat the shot over and over and over—the more they've prepared themselves to complete that shot in a game. Demonstrate that the hoop is actually big enough to fit two balls at the same time; they only need to put in one. And when they're doing the work of preparing themselves by practicing and practicing, they don't need to worry about missing shots, or feel bad when they do. In basketball, players who make 50 percent of their shots in a game are considered to have had a very good game. They've missed half their shots, too, but they had the confidence to take all those shots in the first place.

"That doesn't mean take bad shots," Coach Carroll cautions, "but as I tell the young kids I coach: Never up, never in. You want to prepare yourself so you feel confident about taking shots in a game, and then take them."

Types of Shots

The basic shots are the lay-up, hook shot, jump shot, free throw, and three-point shot.

Lay-Up

The lay-up is the most predominant shot in the game, taken at either side of the basket. It is used on a fast break and used when beating a man on a dribble and taking the ball to the rim. Yet it's another fundamental that is often not taught carefully and correctly in the beginning, and many basketball-playing youths have trouble making a lay-up with either hand. If players can do lay-ups with both hands, they know that they can work their way around the basket, warding off other players, and still have confidence in making the shot. If players work on lay-ups with only their dominant hands, they are limiting themselves and their ability to score; they are allowing themselves to be less of a player.

Jump Shot

The jump shot is the basic shot, the meat and potatoes of basketball. A jump shot can be taken from a fixed position after receiving a pass, on a moving catch, or off a dribble. It opens up the rest of a player's game, and is essential to being a complete basketball player.

Hook Shot

The hook shot is important because it gives a player versatility around the rim and creates space between the ball and the defender. With a lay-up, the player goes in square to the basket, which means the ball may be more available for a defensive swat. With a hook shot, however, the player is at an angle, often warding off the defender with one side of the body and hooking the ball in with the opposite arm and hand. This allows shooters to put themselves and the rim between the ball and the defender.

Free Throw

A free throw from the foul line is the only guaranteed uncontested shot taken during the game of basketball. Some people say that, for this reason, the free throw should be the easiest shot to make. Others say it's the hardest because it's not like any other shot taken in the game, and different factors can come into play, like the crowd and late-game pressure. There's no doubt that thousands of games have been won or lost through free throws. And as many variations as you'll see in, say, the family birthday cake, you'll also see in free-throw-shooting routines. According to Coach Carroll, this is a good thing. But ultimately, the essence of the free throw is not the style of the routine, it's the ability to make the free throw, and that takes consistent concentration.

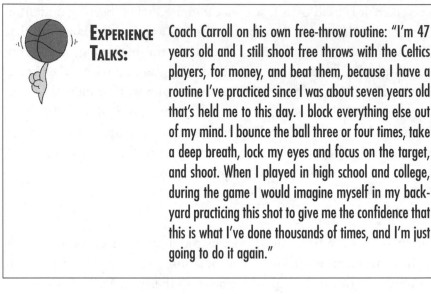

EXPERIENCE TALKS: Coach Carroll on his own free-throw routine: "I'm 47 years old and I still shoot free throws with the Celtics players, for money, and beat them, because I have a routine I've practiced since I was about seven years old that's held me to this day. I block everything else out of my mind. I bounce the ball three or four times, take a deep breath, lock my eyes and focus on the target, and shoot. When I played in high school and college, during the game I would imagine myself in my backyard practicing this shot to give me the confidence that this is what I've done thousands of times, and I'm just going to do it again."

Three-Point Shot

The three-point shot is one made from outside the curved line that extends on both sides from the top of the key to the baseline on either side of the basket; the college or student three-point line is different, and closer to the basket, than the NBA three-point line. Still, the three-point shot, in Coach Carroll's opinion, has been a curse for many young people learning how to shoot. "So many kids are infatuated with the three-point shot. If you can't dunk, you want to make threes. Many kids are shooting threes way before they're strong enough to shoot from that far out, and that can produce a lot of bad habits. You don't need a three-point shot to be a good shooter and help your team."

That said, the three-point shot can be a powerful component of a team's game for one simple reason—math. Let's say the members of a team make half the two-point shots they take. Out of every 10 shots taken, then, they make 5 and rack up 10 points; that's shooting at 50 percent and that's good. But if this same team can make 3 of 10 three-pointers, they've put nine points on the board while only making 30 percent of their shots.

Gauging when a player or team is ready for three-point shots is more about strength than it is about height or age. Some kids in fifth grade may be able to get a three in, but as a coach, ascertain whether they're shooting or hoisting. If they're still hoisting or hurling with more effort than control, they're not strong enough to practice the three with consistent good form.

Shooting Mechanics

Shooting any basketball shot requires the same basic mechanics, with minor variations.

- **Eyes.** The rim of the basket is the target for the ball. Eyes have to be on the rim as early as possible. Players should not be watching their dribble. When a person drives a car, that person is watching the road. Likewise, when driving to the basket, players should already have their eyes on the rim, never on the ball. Eliminate all distractions when shooting; keep eyes focused on that rim.

- **Body.** Power for shooting is generated through the base of the body: legs and feet. In much the way a foundation is built for a house, the foundation for the shot is built here in the body. The body is balanced in athletic or ready position with the feet shoulder width apart and pointing toward the target, knees slightly bent, hips and shoulders square to the target. Coming off legs that are flexed is going to generate power for the shot, which allows the arms to be used for giving touch or finesse to the ball.

- **Hands.** The shooting hand is directly behind the ball with the fingers spread out comfortably on its surface, and the index finger at the midpoint of the ball or on the valve. The hands are relaxed; the ball is on the pads of the fingers, not the palm of the hand. The fingertips offer more control in releasing the ball, the ability to give the ball a "softer touch." *The guide hand, or nondominant hand, is used to support the ball and is not actually involved in shooting the ball.* The guide hand is flat, like a pancake, held against the side of the ball to guide the ball, and comes off right before the shot is released. Most beginning players want to use both hands to shoot, but this complicates the mechanics by adding a second power source and the need to synchronize directional pushes from two different places. Shooting, at its most efficient and accurate, is a one-hand activity.

⚫ **Arm.** The shooting arm forms an L, with the elbow bent and held at around chest height close to the body to hold the ball comfortably aloft somewhere between the shoulder and ear, like a waiter carrying a tray. The elbow is pointed at the target of the rim, like a dart to a bull's-eye.

The synchronization of all these moving parts makes the shot. As the knees straighten, the back and shoulders engage to put power behind the shooting arm. In one smooth motion, the hand pushes up and over, and, as the guide hand comes off, the shooting wrist flexes and the fingers push to put a soft backspin on the ball. The hand, still pointing to the target, completes the arc and comes down as if reaching into a cookie jar.

Shooting mechanics sequence.

Shooting mechanics sequence (continued).

Drills

1. FORM SHOOTING

This drill practices the basic shooting motion described above with just the shooting hand, no guide hand. It is a good warm-up drill for all ages.

In athletic or ready stance, take the ball in hand, spread the fingers apart, and hold the ball aloft like a waiter holding a tray. With eyes on the target and the ball balanced on the fingertips, reach up and over to shoot the ball into the basket, finishing with a hand in the cookie jar. Start right in front of the basket, working on getting the ball to arc up and over the rim, finishing with a strong follow-through and keeping the body balanced from start to finish. Line up two to three players at a basket, and have them each shoot for about a minute at a time before going to the end of the line.

Setting the ball.

STEP IT UP: Make 5 to 10 baskets in a row; move back two steps; then four steps; and so on.

DURATION: 5–10 minutes, depending upon number of baskets and number of players.

2. TWO-HAND FORM SHOOTING

This is a variation on the drill above using the guide hand. Prepare as above, only this time position the guide hand along the side of the ball. The hand is flat and is stabilizing the ball, but not holding it. Players practice the rhythm of removing the guide hand right before the snap of the wrist and release of the ball.

DURATION: 5–10 minutes.

3. SHOOT FOR THE STARS

Lie on the back on the floor, the body still except for the dominant hand balancing a ball on the fingertips in ready-to-shoot position. Extend the arm and follow through straight up, then catch the ball as it comes down. Kids have to really focus on squaring their body and shooting straight or the ball will not come down anywhere near where it went up and they will not be able to catch it. A variation is to sit in a chair with the ball balanced between shoulder and ear, and extending the arm, sending the ball up, following through, then catching the ball in the same hand.

Shooting for the stars.

4. TWO-LINE SHOOTING

Divide the team in half and line the kids up in two facing lines 5 to 10 feet apart, depending upon age and strength; they should be able to get the ball comfortably to each other without straining. Identify partners in facing lines. Partners "shoot" to each other, using correct form and follow-through. This drill can also be done against the wall with players rebounding their own ball off the wall as it comes back to them, and "shooting" again.

5. SHOOTING THE LAY-UP

The key to the lay-up is learning how to jump. A player begins working on lay-ups with the dominant hand. If this is the right hand, the player is jumping off the left foot. Starting tight to the right side of the basket, the left foot on the ground, the right knee raised up in the air, extend the ball up as high as possible with the right hand before flexing the wrist and releasing the ball. The target is the square on the backboard; the goal is to bank or "kiss" the ball off the middle of this square and into the basket. For left-handers, start on the left side of the basket, the right foot on the ground, the left knee up, the ball ready in the left hand.

Lay-up, jumping off the correct foot.

STEP IT UP: Back up a step to shoot a little farther away from the basket. Then try a lay-up with a step: For instance, for a right-hander, start with the right foot on the ground, step onto the left, bring the right knee up, and release the shot as above. This can be increased so players are taking a couple steps and a dribble before releasing. Practice the same sequences with the nondominant hand.

DURATION: 5–10 minutes when practicing various variations.

6. SHOOTING THE JUMP SHOT

Players line up behind the foul line. The first player comes to a point about 8 to 10 feet in front of the basket and stands in ready position, the same foot as his dominant hand slightly forward, knees bent, hands at chest height ready to catch the ball. The coach passes the ball to the player. As the player catches it, he jumps up, raising the knee on his nondominant side, and shoots the ball. This player rebounds his own ball, returns it to the coach, goes to the end of the line, the next player takes a shot, and so forth. Once the kids have the mechanics of the shot, they can break off into partners, to take turns being the shooter and the passer. Two groups can be working, with the passers on each side of the basket feeding the shooters.

STEP IT UP: Take the shots from farther back, or from the sides.

DURATION: 5 minutes.

Jump shot, the correct form.

7. JUMP SHOT ON THE MOVE

Every time players shoot a jump shot, you as coach want them to be re-creating the fundamental position and mechanics that they practiced standing still. This becomes harder to do when they begin moving into the shot. When learning jump shots on the move, have your players take an extra moment to center themselves and get in position before shooting.

Players are lined up around the foul line, one player out in front of the basket, the coach on the side ready to pass. The first player takes two steps to the right with hands staying in ready position. The coach throws the player the ball; the player pivots on the inside foot to square to the basket, and takes a jump shot. This player gets the ball and returns it to the coach; the next player shoots; et cetera. After the line goes through with steps to the right, repeat with steps to the left.

> **STEP IT UP:** Invert the drill. The coach is now at the foul line, while the player stands with back to the basket and takes steps away from the basket. Upon catching the ball, the player plants the inside foot, pivots to the basket, squares up, and shoots.
>
> **DURATION:** 5 minutes.

8. LEARNING THE HOOK SHOT

This drill is taken from the practice routine of 6-foot, 10-inch George Mikan, who entered the NBA in 1949 and became the first successful big man, leading the league in scoring for six straight years. This drill practices footwork, but it is especially critical that younger kids use lower baskets and smaller balls so they can do the drill and not be straining and hoisting to maneuver the ball. Players can line up behind the foul line, with the first player coming in front of the basket. To learn this drill, have players work solely with the dominant hand until they get the move. The player starts in the ready position holding the ball at chest height. A right-hander shifts her weight to her left foot, using her knees to push off while her right knee comes up, then jumps and hooks the ball into the basket with her right hand. Left-handers would use the opposite sequence. Once players understand the move, the drill is to do this first on the right side, then on the left, and back and forth for 30 seconds. Then the next person in line does the drill, back and forth, right hook then left hook, for 30 seconds.

Shooting the hook shot.

STEP IT UP: Move farther back so players are no longer taking hook lay-ups, or add dribbles, staying on one side and shooting several times, then switching to the other side and shooting several times (for this variation, don't go back and forth with every shot).

Players in Group III can do this drill starting with their feet straddling the box, their backs to the basket, then take one or two hard dribbles into the paint and shoot.

DURATION: 5–10 minutes.

9. FREE-THROW SHOOTING

When teaching distance shooting, be sure to stress the use of the legs to your young players. Children do not have the same chest and arm strength that adults do, and—especially as they begin to get fatigued later in a game—they need to use the more powerful muscles of their legs to maintain their control, their power, and their ability to get the ball to the target.

Most players stand behind the line with the same foot as their dominant hand slightly forward, knees bent. After a dribble, or a breath, or whatever each player decides, using the correct shooting technique, concentrating, eyes on the basket, the player takes the shot. Once the correct shot has been taught, use as many baskets as you have and start by having every player take at least 10 foul shots at every practice. (Younger players generally start a few steps ahead of the foul line with a lower basket and smaller ball.)

STEP IT UP: Decide on a goal of making so many shots per 10—say, 3 or 4 out of 10. As players' abilities increase, the goal can be making 8 out of 10; once more than 2 shots are missed in such a sequence, players start over again until they can achieve 8 out of 10 free throws. You can also make this a swish drill with so many swish foul shots made, or practice shooting with eyes closed. For a team foul-shooting drill for older players, each player takes one or two shots and as a team they have to shoot a certain percentage—say, 75 percent.

DURATION: 5–10 minutes.

10. LAY-UP WITH DRIBBLE MOVES

A quality one-on-one player is able to shoot off the dribble. This drill works on using dribble moves into a lay-up or short jump shot. The team is divided into two groups. Position a cone or coach on each of the elbows of the key and line up the two lines a few steps behind this point. Have at least two balls for each line, or every player can have a ball. The first player in each line dribbles at and then around the obstacle—tight to the cone, or shoulder to shoulder to the coach—then continues dribbling to finish with a lay-up. Switch lines so players shooting right-hand lay-ups are now on the left side shooting left-hand lay-ups. Then finish the drill with a short jump shot.

STEP IT UP: Use different dribble moves to come into the shot, such as a stutter, crossover stutter, crossover inside out, or spin dribble.

DURATION: 10 minutes.

11. PIVOT SHOOTING

With his back to the basket, the starting player throws the ball to himself, using a backspin lob toss, releasing the ball with a backspin so it comes right back into his hands. Keeping one foot in place, the player pivots to face the basket and takes a shot using one of the following pivots:

   Inside pivot. Jump-stop, then pivot on the inside foot (the foot toward the basket) 180 degrees in the direction toward the basket to a triple-threat position.

Reverse pivot. Jump-stop, then pivot on the inside foot 180 degrees the other way to square to the basket.

Jumpstop (left).

Pivoting (right).

STEP IT UP: When beginning the drill, the coach can choose which pivot players have to execute. For more advanced players, the coach can call out the pivot as each player releases the pass to himself.

DURATION: 5 minutes.

12. ONE-DRIBBLE JUMP SHOT

The team lines up behind the foul line, one ball for the player at the head of the line, one ball for the player beginning the drill. The player starts 8 feet in front of the basket with a basketball. A right-handed player takes one dribble to the right and plants the right foot, then does a hard dribble that brings the ball up into the hand while planting the left foot. Pivot on the left foot, plant the right foot square to the basket, head up, eyes on the rim, and shoot. The first player gets the ball, gives it to the second person in line, and returns to the end of the line while the other player with the ball begins the drill.

STEP IT UP: Move farther from the basket, or take two dribbles.

DURATION: 5–10 minutes.

13. SPOT SHOOTING

Player C under the basket is the rebounder. Player B on the side is the passer. Player A starting on the elbow is the shooter. C and B each start with a ball. B passes to A, and A squares her body to the basket and takes a jump shot from the elbow, then runs to the other elbow, receives another pass from B—who has received C's ball on a pass—squares to the basket, and takes a jump shot. Two balls are used so A is constantly shooting for 30 seconds as C rebounds the ball and passes to B and B passes to A. Then the players rotate and the next player shoots for 30 seconds; then the last rotation is made, and the third player shoots. Repeat the sequence, this time with the players shooting from the point where the foul line extends to intersect with the three-point line—the elbow bank; and then where the elbow bank extends to intersect with the baseline—the bank corner.

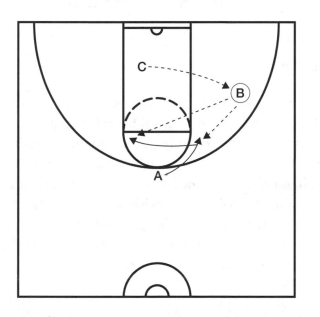

DURATION: 5 minutes.

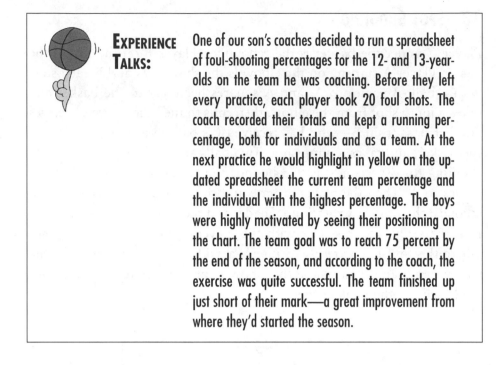

EXPERIENCE TALKS: One of our son's coaches decided to run a spreadsheet of foul-shooting percentages for the 12- and 13-year-olds on the team he was coaching. Before they left every practice, each player took 20 foul shots. The coach recorded their totals and kept a running percentage, both for individuals and as a team. At the next practice he would highlight in yellow on the updated spreadsheet the current team percentage and the individual with the highest percentage. The boys were highly motivated by seeing their positioning on the chart. The team goal was to reach 75 percent by the end of the season, and according to the coach, the exercise was quite successful. The team finished up just short of their mark—a great improvement from where they'd started the season.

14. SWISH DRILL

The object of this drill is to make a basket without hitting the rim, thereby making the net "swish." This is harder than just getting the ball in and requires the shooter to really concentrate on directing and sending that ball. This can be done as a single-hand drill or with both hands, the shooting hand with the guide hand in place. Start right in front of a basket with a starting goal of two swishes, then the player goes to the end of the line and the next player is up. If several baskets are used and players get back up quickly, the next goal could be two swishes in a row, three swishes, three swishes in a row, et cetera.

STEP IT UP: Begin to step back farther from the basket and/or increase the number of swish baskets made in a row. With older kids, you can use a scoring system of plus one for a swish, minus one for a miss, and zero for a basket that goes in but hits the rim. Each player then shoots the same number of times; the one with the most points wins.

DURATION: 10 minutes.

15. TWO-BALL SHOOTING

For this drill, there are three players—one shooter, one rebounder, one passer—and two balls. Coaches can pick out the spots to shoot from, taking the age and ability of the team into account. Younger players might shoot five shots each from the two boxes, the two elbows, and the foul line. Older players can shoot 10 shots each from the corners, the elbows, and the top of the key.

Player A shoots the first ball. Player B then throws him the second ball while Player C rebounds the first ball. Player A shoots the second ball. C then throws the first ball to B. B passes A the first ball again, and A shoots again. The players rotate through the first spot, then on to the next, and so on.

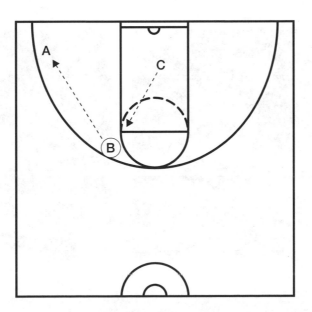

DURATION: 10–20 minutes.

16. TRIPLE-THREAT SHOOTING

The triple-threat position is one where the player is crouched, knees bent, body balanced over the feet, ball held in two hands up in front of the chest. From this position the player can go right, left, or straight ahead. The goal of this drill is to enhance the player's ability to take a shot off a left dribble, right dribble, or forward dribble, without compromising the basics of the actual shot.

Players will be in one line around the top of the key. The location where the first player will actually start the drill is determined by age and strength. Once again, make sure the players are close enough and the basket is low enough that they are not straining to shoot. The second player in line goes under the basket to rebound. The first player begins by taking a step and one hard dribble to the right. On a hard dribble, the bounce is pushed down a little harder so the ball comes back harder and higher and better positioned to take up and into a shot. Then the left foot is planted and the body squared to the basket. As the ball returns up into the player's hand, the guide hand comes in to lock the ball in shooting position, and the player finishes the shot. The first player takes 10 shots to the right, then 10 shots to the left. Then the shooter takes the rebounder's position and the rebounder shoots. The next two come up and repeat the drill.

Triple threat position (left).

One hard dribble (right).

STEP IT UP: Take the shots farther from the basket, or increase the number of dribbles before the shot.

DURATION: 5–10 minutes.

17. Two-Ball Alternate Shooting

Player A is near the basket; players B and C are farther away at the base of a triangle of which A is the point. A shoots the ball from any spot and gets her own rebound while C sprints to whatever spot she would like to shoot from. A throws her rebounded ball to C. In the meantime, B has shot a ball and rebounded. A sprints to where she wants to shoot, and B throws her the ball. C has shot and rebounded the ball and now throws that ball to B in position, and the pattern continues.

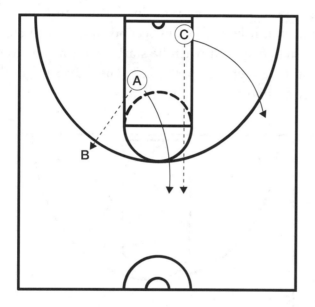

Duration: 5 minutes.

18. Three-Point Shooting

For three-point shots, have players take one to two steps into a balanced position and then lift up from a crouch to get the power to send the shot the distance. Start with half the team under the basket and half in the middle of the court at the three-point line. Player A under the basket throws the ball to player B as B steps to the three-point line with legs bent, and takes the shot. Then B rebounds, A goes to end of line B, and the drill continues.

Duration: 5–10 minutes.

Games

1. AROUND THE WORLD

Spots are chosen to make shots all around the basket, often three in front in the paint and another seven around the arc. Spots can be named using cities from around the world. Have at least two players at each basket. The first player begins at the first spot. If he makes it, he goes on to the next, et cetera. If he misses, he can stop his turn there and start at the same basket when he's up again—or he can take a chance and take a second shot. If he makes this second shot, he can continue. If he misses, his turn is over and when he starts again he has to start at the beginning. Only once chance per round. The player to get the farthest, or all the way around the world first, wins.

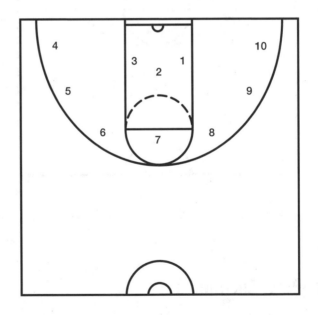

DURATION: 10 minutes.

2. HORSE OR OUT

At least two to four players per basket is a good number for this game. The first person takes a shot from any spot. If she makes it, the next person has to shoot from that space. If the next person misses, she gets the letter *H*, or *O*, and the person after her can take a shot from anywhere. The game continues—if Erin makes the shot, then Meg behind her has to make the shot from the same place; if Meg misses, she gets a letter. When a player gets all the letters *H-O-R-S-E*, or *O-U-T*, she's out of the game. The winner is the last person in.

DURATION: 10 minutes.

3. KNOCKOUT

Two people or more line up at the foul line at a basket. The first two, Austin and Sean, each have a ball. Austin shoots from the foul line. If Austin makes it, he gets the ball, gives it to the third person in line, Kevin, and goes to the end of the line. Sean shoots and does the same if he makes it. If Sean misses, he rebounds the ball and continues to shoot from anywhere while Kevin behind him can now start the game by taking a free throw. Once there are two people shooting on the basket, the first person to make the basket goes to the end of the line; the person shooting is out. The next two start and the game progresses until only one person is left in.

DURATION: 10 minutes.

4. GREAT ALASKAN SHOOT-OUT

The object of this popular game is to make as many baskets as possible at the point (or money) basket. In order to progress to the point basket, a team must keep winning the shoot-outs at the other baskets, and thereby keep moving around the circuit. The team that wins at the point basket racks up points, and stays to compete there again.

Generally, the game is played with teams of two to four players using somewhere between three and seven baskets. At each basket, the coach marks two lines with masking tape, evenly on either side of the basket. For the shot to be counted, the shooter's feet must be behind this line when the shot is made. The line can be the same for every basket, or it can be different. For beginning players, the shots could be lay-ups, with no floor marking.

The two teams competing at each of the baskets line up behind the line. Coach blows the whistle and gives the teams 30 to 60 seconds (whatever duration is chosen, keep it consistent throughout the game) to make baskets. The first player in line shoots once, gets the rebound, passes to the next teammate in line, and goes to the end. The second player shoots, rebounds, goes to the end, and the pattern continues. When the second whistle blows, the team that made the most shots proceeds to the next basket. The team that wins at the point basket, however, stays, with the losing team proceeding to the next basket. Every time a team wins at the point basket, they get one point; the coach is stationed here keeping score. When time is up, the coach adds up points made at the point basket and that team wins the shoot-out.

Duration: 10–15 minutes.

Experience Talks:

This is an extremely popular basketball camp game, with some camps actually giving money out to the winners—hence the name *money basket*. Generally speaking, the game is played with the teams keeping track of their own points everywhere except the point basket, where a coach keeps score with a clipboard. As the kids get older, or if there are several players on a team, this tends to work itself out—too many of the players know what's going on and are watching and keeping track of the other team for there to be much discrepancy in counts. The younger your players, however, the more likely it is that sustained arguments will crop up over foot violations, incorrect basket counts, and players not going to the end of the line—that is, the better shooters ending up with the ball more than the other players on their team. (Caught up in the fervor, many teammates will go along with this in pursuit of the win.) If you have an extra coach, an older son or daughter, or parents sitting around watching or showing up early for pickup, position one to monitor each basket, and make their count final; no appeals!

CHAPTER 7

THE ART OF OFFENSE

Playing basketball is about action and reaction. You do Y, your defender does X, you counter with Z; or maybe your teammate counters with Z; or maybe two of your teammates counter with Z+, and so forth. When teaching offense, this is the spirit you as a coach want to maintain; you want to teach your players how to act and react.

So face up to these facts: You have not been tapped to this youth coaching position to live out fantasies of leading virtual robots through an offensive playbook that illustrates your brilliant strategic abilities.

"Since I've been watching youth basketball, I've been amazed at how few youth coaches are able to teach offensive basketball," says Coach Carroll. "I'm bewildered by their emphasis on running set plays that are so limiting. By focusing on sets, the kids are not learning how to play basketball. If a young person learns how to play basketball, he or she can run any set. But if this same player practices mostly sets, he or she is lost outside of a set. I was watching a youth game once where the team was running an out-of-bounds play. One of the players on offense managed to break to the basket and was wide open. His teammate out-of-bounds with the ball was so fixated on running the play, he never saw the opportunity staring him in the face; he never threw it to the open man and they missed the opportunity for an easy, uncontested lay-up."

Running plays is a crutch for coaches who are not able to teach kids how to play offensive basketball, believes Coach Carroll—a crutch you are not going to need. This section is designed to give you, the coach, what you need to teach the basics of offense, to build the ladder that will take your team to a high level of offensive basketball.

Preparing for the Climb

Another myth to shatter before even contemplating the first rung of this ladder is the idea of positions. "To label kids as forwards, centers, point guards, et cetera, is gibberish when they're growing up," says Coach Carroll. "You don't know when they're going to stop growing, or what they're going to be able to do as a mature player. As a youth coach, you want to maximize every kid's abilities in every facet of the game. Winning a game with a second-grade team is inconsequential if it's achieved at the expense of developing your players' abilities. Until high school, like clothes that are unisex, think of developing players with uniskills. Support your players in playing all positions."

An overall concept of offensive basketball that you can introduce to your young players first is that of spacing. In order to maximize the possibilities of the five players on the court, players need to have approximately 15 feet of spacing between each other. Help your players imagine a string attaching them all, or literally make a string or rope with markers at each 15 feet and let them hold on to this length at the markers and experience how far apart from each other they want to be. This kind of spacing puts pressure on the defense in terms of guarding the ball and makes it easier for the offense to cut, pass, or drive to the basket.

Starting Up the Offensive Ladder

Get in Position

In order to pose a threat to the defensive team, the offensive team needs to be able to get something started, or initiated, in the scoring areas. In theory, all offensive players should be positioned so that at any point they can catch the ball and be ready to score. As kids get bigger and stronger and can shoot from farther out, these scoring areas will, of course, expand. So the first step of initiating an offense means players are able to handle the basketball to effectively get in position, from point A to point B, through either dribbling or passing.

This can be a difficult piece to coach since, until they reach high school age, many players may understand the concept but lack the dribbling and passing abilities that allow them to execute it. Here again is where drills build the confidence of skill and experience that will help them in the pressure situation of a game.

EXPERIENCE TALKS: A very common sight in youth basketball games is the singular positioning of the "giant," the young boy or girl who's sometimes a head taller than most of the other players. The coach stands this child under the basket to shoot or rebound, period. That team usually wins, but in terms of developing abilities, everybody in this scenario loses.

Get Open

Once positioned, players need to be able to get open, getting free of any defenders who are pressuring and in the way of the offense. One of the best ways to get open is the V-cut. A V-cut is exactly what it sounds like: The offensive player runs or cuts in one direction to take his defender that way, then changes direction to V off another way and keep his defender off balance, freeing himself up.

To make a V-cut, the player runs her defender down, then, in athletic position with knees flexed, she cuts off her defender's path by stepping one leg in front of her defender's body. Then going into triple-threat position, she cuts off in the other direction (making the V) with a hand up as a target for a pass, leaving her defender behind her. She can then catch the pass and square up to shoot.

Get Moving

The hardest offense to guard is one where the players are moving with a purpose. A player who stands still is much easier to guard than one who is moving. In addition, his defender is freed up to disrupt other offensive players. Moving and cutting is a critical part of offensive basketball, but there is a fine and—often to players—fuzzy line between moving and moving with a purpose. When a player passes, thereby releasing the ball to a teammate, he has three solid options:

1. **Cut to the basket.** This creates an opportunity to get a return pass and score. If this player doesn't receive a pass, he keeps moving to create adequate spacing.

2. **Cut away from the ball.** This takes one defender, and one player, away from the ball, creating more space for teammates.

3. **Cut and come back.** This, often termed "replace yourself," moves the defender and renews the threat to this defender that this player could now have opened himself to receive the ball.

EXPERIENCE TALKS: If a player passes and goes to the ball, this generally achieves nothing. In fact, this maneuver hurts the offense from a spacing aspect, creating congestion with four players around the ball.

Basic Offensive Rungs

A very basic, but effective, framework to take your team's basketball game to a high level consists of the following techniques:

- Backdoor cut.
- Flash.
- Give and go.
- Downscreen.
- Backscreen.
- Pick and roll.

These are the fundamental components of team basketball, and will be developed in the drills that follow. Truly understanding these moves is what will take your players' game to the next level. For these techniques are not set plays or set calls, but practiced movements conducted by subsets of the five players on a team in response to reading the defender. *One of the single most important aspects of offensive basketball is this ability to read the defense.* Many high school and college coaches spend an entire season doing nothing but preparing and coaching their team to read the defense; it's that critical to successfully playing the game. If you as a coach can instruct your players in how to read their defenders, this single skill will go a long way toward raising their ability as basketball players and, more often than not, will put them in the middle of the action. Here's why: A player who focuses on being the best she can be in reading her defender, instead of worrying about the ball and how to get it into her own hands, will discover that the ball begins to find her; soon she's right in the middle of the offense, even though she hasn't directly searched out the ball at all.

Offensive Drills

1. Spacing Drill

Put five kids on a half court approximately 15 feet apart. Have them pass around the perimeter in order to get a sense of what 15 feet is. Then readjust by putting one player in the middle, with the players around the perimeter still all 15 feet from each other and from the middle player. Continue passing in an established order.

> **Step It Up:** Have the player make a V-cut before catching the ball and then squaring up and taking a triple-threat position. Then expand the sequence to a V-cut, catch, triple threat, one or two dribbles, and then pass.

2. V-Cut Drill

The team is in two lines above the foul line extended; the drill runs simultaneously on both sides. Have cones or markers set up off the box on each side, with a player from each line in the wing a few steps off the cone. To start the drill, player B on the wing runs at the cones, then V-cuts away to catch a pass from player A, the first person in line. B catches the ball and assumes a triple-threat position. B then rotates to the end of the line, A becomes B, and a new A takes the ball. Once the players are through their line, the lines switch sides to run the drill on the opposite side of the basket.

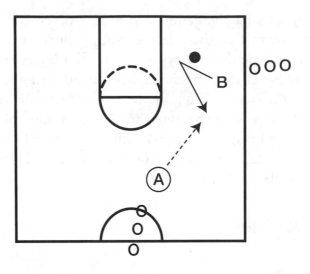

3. GIVE-AND-GO DRILL

Give and go is to the game of basketball what bread and butter used to be to dinner: No game would be even considered a game without plenty of it. The give is the pass from one player to another; the go is the actual cut to the basket. When a player makes the pass, he must set up his defender by taking him in one direction or another before making a cut to the basket. Set up roughly the same as in the V-cut drill. This time player A initiates the offense by starting back at the half-court line and making a hard dribble toward the cone. Player B V-cuts on the side; A passes to B and cuts to the basket, then clears out, running an arc away from the basket. Players rotate, and the drill continues through one line. Then the lines switch sides.

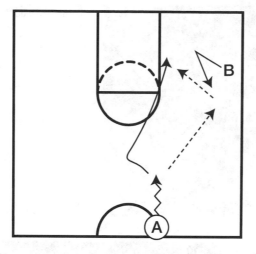

STEP IT UP: When A cuts to the basket, B passes to A and A makes a lay-up.

DURATION: 5–10 minutes.

4. BACKDOOR CUT

The backdoor is an important technique to use for getting open. This can be used by an offensive player when she is being pressured or when she has the ball on the wing and wants to cut to the basket. If she doesn't back down, the defender(s) can keep pressing her more and more; this is a quick reverse in direction designed to give her some relief. The setup is roughly the same as in previous drills. Player B V-cuts by taking a step or two back away from the play, then plants her foot, with her hand out to receive a

pass in a decoy move. B then pivots on the balls of her feet, pushes off her back foot, and goes toward the basket, staying low, her hand out as a target again. Player A delivers a bounce pass to B. Rotate players through the line, then switch sides.

Setting up the backdoor cut.

Cutting backdoor.

Completing the backdoor cut.

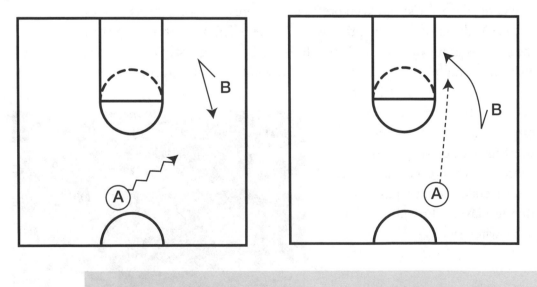

DURATION: 5–10 minutes.

5. FLASH DRILL

A flash is a movement by someone away from the basketball to a clear space nearer the basketball. A flash is used to relieve pressure on the ball handler or another teammate being denied the basketball. A flash can not only help a teammate, but also be an offensive weapon itself because it can create a backdoor opportunity for a teammate, who then flashes to the ball open to receive the pass.

Three players are involved in this drill. Player A is behind the elbow, B is in the wing, and C is behind the baseline. C flashes up to the elbow with hands up, calling "Flash," while B does a V-cut. A throws a chest pass to C. As C catches the ball, B cuts backdoor and C throws B a bounce pass for a lay-up. The team can be divided into three groups, lined up at these positions. The lines then rotate to the next position. When all positions have been played, repeat this drill on the opposite side.

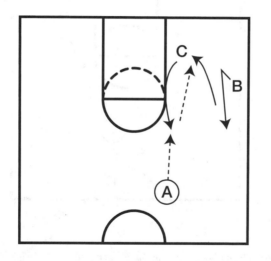

DURATION: 5–10 minutes.

6. V-CUT SHOOTING

Being able to shoot off offensive moves is an important fundamental. The ability to move and create space to get a shot off will increase offensive players' scoring ability.

The team is divided into two lines near the half-court line, a passing line and a shooting line. The first two players in each line start with the first one on the side of the basket—the shooter; and the second one above the key—the passer. Everyone in the passing line has a ball. (For young players, the passer can be a coach.) A coach or cone is stationed between the two on each side. The shooter takes a couple of steps toward the basket and then makes a V-cut move back around the coach or cone toward the passer. The player's body is low, knees bent, body squared, hands up to receive the pass. The passer releases the ball to the shooter, who catches the ball, squares to the basket, and shoots the ball. The shooter rebounds the ball, then shooter and passer finish at the end of the line. When the line is finished, the lines reverse sides and repeat the drill.

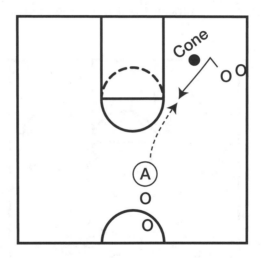

STEP IT UP: This drill can begin close to the basket so the shooter finishes with a lay-up. To make the drill more involved, change the starting position of the shooter and the position of the cone or coach to enable one dribble into a lay-up, a longer dribble into a lay-up, or a dribble into a short jump shot.

DURATION: 5–10 minutes.

7. Downscreen Drill/8. Backscreen Drill

A screen is when a player takes his body and positions himself in such a way that he blocks the path of a defender guarding a teammate. In order to make the screen most effective, the player must have the proper angle. In setting a downscreen, a player lines up his body so his back is to the basketball. In setting a backscreen, a player lines up his body so that his back is to the rim. Setting screens is an effective way to get a teammate open for a shot, but many times the player setting the screen also opens himself up because his defender may follow the cutter to the basket.

But effectively setting the screen is just the beginning. To utilize a screen, the player who has the screen set for him must know how to read his defender and then execute the proper cut. This player coming off the screen has four basic options:

A. **Straight cut.** This is used when a defender is trying to fight through a screen. Here the player V-cuts then comes off the screen, shoulder to shoulder, ready to catch the basketball.

B. **Curl.** The player V-cuts, then curls over the screen to the basket.

C. **Backcut.** The player V-cuts, comes to the screen, then goes backdoor.

D   **Fade.** The player V-cuts, comes to the screen, then fades back one or two steps away from the screen.

Downscreen Drill

To set up this drill, player A is off the elbow toward half court. C is on the wing. B is off the other elbow. Player B V-cuts to receive the ball. A throws B the ball. A sets a downscreen on C. C comes straight up off the screen to receive the ball from B, then dribbles in to the basket to shoot. Or C curls, backcuts, or fades off the screen to receive the ball; choose one per practice.

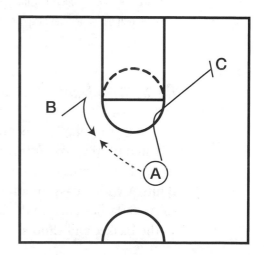

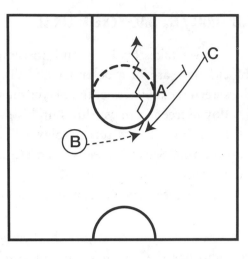

STEP IT UP: Put defense on the court. The first option is just to have dummy defense, which means that the defensive players basically just stand in the way.

A second option is that player C doesn't receive the pass. Instead A pops back toward the ball; B throws the ball to A; A catches the ball and shoots or drives. (This re-creates what happens in a game when two defenders are guarding a downscreen. Sometimes the cutter is the man who may be open; sometimes the screener may be open.)

A third option is to have A receive the ball. With the same beginning format, A throws B the ball; A sets a screen for C; C straight-cuts to the ball. But B does not pass to C. Instead A backcuts to the basket, and B throws A the ball.

DURATION: 10–15 minutes. (Choose one or two facets of this drill to work on per practice. Depending upon the age and experience of your team, introducing and working through all the different aspects implicated in this drill may be a two-season process.)

BACKSCREEN DRILL

For this drill, player A is on the wing, B is at the top of the key, and C is a step off the box. A throws B the ball. C sets a backscreen with back to the rim. A takes C right then cuts off left, or left then cuts off right. B hits A with a pass for a lay-up. A second option is that B does not pass to A. C flashes back to the ball. B throws C the ball. C shoots, or drives to the basket and shoots.

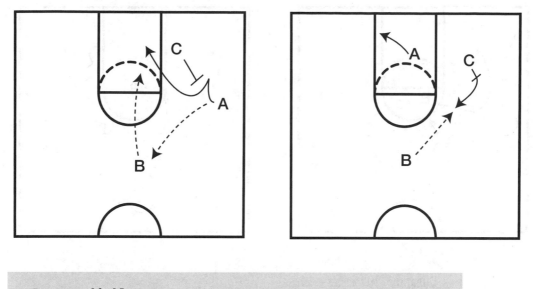

DURATION: 10–15 minutes.

9. PICK AND ROLL

The pick and roll is one of the only phases of offensive basketball where a teammate coming to the ball is helpful. The pick is the screen, only this time the screen is on the ball. The dribbler comes off the screen, shoulder to shoulder with the screener, not allowing room for the defender to slide in between. The dribbler is trying to turn the corner around the screen, lower her shoulder, and drive to the basket, possibly for her own shot; to take a jump shot; or to create penetration for a pass to a teammate. The screener then rolls to the basket, and the dribbler may be able to hit her with a pass for a lay-up.

To set up, player A is just in front of the center circle. B comes up and sets a screen on the ball. A can come off to the right or to the left. B then rolls by pivoting and opening her body to maintain vision of the basketball, and moves to the basket. A can drive to the basket for a lay-up, shoot a short jump shot, or hit B with a bounce pass. This is a middle pick. Pairs can switch positions, then a new pair can rotate in.

This variation practices a side pick. This time A dribbles to the foul line extended. B sprints out and sets a pick. A drives off, keeping shoulder to shoulder, looking for a lay-up, short jump shot, or bounce pass to B, who has rolled to the basket. This drill can be performed first to one side, then the other.

DURATION: 10 minutes.

Individual Offensive Moves

Offensive basketball begins and ends with one-on-one play. If players do not have the ability to beat their man in a one-on-one situation, their efforts on offense are ultimately going to be unsuccessful. Previous sections have discussed beating a defender off the dribble, and how to get a shot off screens and cuts. There are, however, many times when an offensive player will catch the ball off either a cut or a screen and not have an initial shot. At this point, a player wants to get into a triple-threat position, square to the basket, and counter the defender's efforts with various footwork moves. These moves are called the jab step series.

The jab step allows players to attack a defender with hard foot fakes to get the defender off balance and create an opening to either shoot the jumper or drive the ball right or left to the basket. This series allows players to create their own shot.

Jab Step Series

To initiate the jab step, the player starts in a triple-threat position, then takes a hard short step forward on the dominant foot at the defender. With head up, eyes on the basket, the player is protecting the ball by holding it over the dominant hip, in a balanced stance, now with the dominant foot slightly ahead of the other foot. The goal of this move is to get the opponent back on his or her heels.

Next, off this jab step, there are three possibilities in this series:

1. **Jab, jump shot.** If the defender backs up, the player goes right into a jump shot.

2. **Jab and go.** If the defender doesn't move when the player jabs, the player pushes off the back foot then takes the dominant foot, extends it farther out by the defender, and moves forward, shoulder to shoulder, in as straight a line to the basket as possible, to go in for a lay-up. *Players need to realize that they have to dribble before they pick up their back foot or this is a walk.*

Triple threat position.

3. **Jab and rip through.** If, when the player jabs, the defender leans in toward the player's dominant hand, the player rips the ball over to the nondominant side, then takes the dominant foot and steps across the opponent's body to go by on the opposite side and in for a lay-up. This is similar to the jab and go, but the player has brought the ball across the body in order to go around the opposite side of the opponent. Again, *the player must dribble before picking up the back foot.*

Jab Series Drills

1. JAB STEP

Line players up in a straight line, each with a ball, and let them work on going from a triple-threat position to a short quick jab step, staying in balance. You want to hear the sound of sneakers squeaking as the players' feet hit the floor hard.

DURATION: 5 minutes.

2. Jab and Jump Shot

Place a cone 5 feet in front of the basket with the players in line at the end of the key. Each player takes a jab and jump shot at the basket and goes to the end of the line. Go through the line a few times.

Step It Up: Move the cone out to 10 feet, then out to 15 feet.

Duration: 5 minutes.

3. Jab and Go

Put a cone near the foul line with players lined up behind the foul line. Players each take a turn jabbing at the cone, then go to right, take one or two dribbles to the basket, and take a shot. Go through the line a few times. (If you have left-handers, have them do this drill to the left.)

Jab step (left).

Jab and go (right).

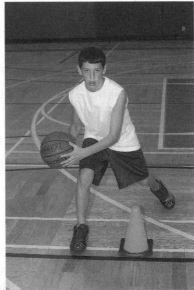

Step It Up: Put the cones in different locations.

Duration: 5 minutes.

4. JAB AND RIP THROUGH

Set up the drill as the jab and go, only this time each player jabs at the cone, rips the ball across to the left, takes one or two dribbles to the basket, and shoots. Go through the line a few times. (Left-handers would be bringing the ball across to their right side and going around the right.)

Jab and rip through.

STEP IT UP: Put the cones in different locations.

DURATION: 5 minutes.

5. JAB WITH DEFENDER

Designate various spots on the court—for instance, elbows, wings, baseline. Have two lines on either side behind the foul line. The first player in each line stands on the elbow. The second player has to make whatever move you designate at this defender: jab and jump shot; jab and go; jab and rip through. The pair then moves on to the wing, and then to the baseline; they can change positions so the defender is now doing the jab step, and come back up to the foul line. Then the next pairs on both sides can do the series.

STEP IT UP: Make the drill "live"—the defensive player plays defense rather than just standing still.

DURATION: 8–10 minutes.

Games

1. GOLF

Each "hole" consists of making a set move from a set spot to make the basket. Before the game, set up how many holes there will be, what they'll be, and where. Six is a good number of holes for younger players; older players can play nine. (You can lower this number depending upon how much practice time you have available.) Draw from the different offensive moves your team has practiced to design the holes; sequences and moves can be repeated on opposite sides of the basket. Decide how many players you want at each basket; with older players, you may decide to put more at each basket, because they often enjoy watching the match as it unfolds. Players keep track of how many attempts it takes them to make the shot—a coach or another player can keep the scorecard. As in golf, the lowest number per hole wins. Each player's final score is tallied by adding all the strokes, or attempts, to make the baskets. The person with the fewest "strokes" wins.

An option for younger players is to play match golf: A player wins a hole by having the fewest strokes, and the final tally counts how many holes each golfer won. This is a good version for younger players, because it will allow someone to come out on top by winning the most amount of holes, without keeping an overall tally that could show some very high scores for players not making baskets easily at any hole.

DURATION: 10–25 minutes.

2. OFFENSIVE MOVES

Divide your players up into equal numbers at however many baskets you have. Let's say you have four baskets and 12 kids; you'll have 3 at each basket. Set a cone up at the elbows. One teammate is the passer on the wing; the other team members are in line behind the foul line. When you blow the whistle, the passer on the wing passes to the first person in line; he dribbles to the cone, jab-steps, and goes in to make a lay-up. He then stays to rebound or get the ball and pass to the person who was behind him; the passer now has to run to take his place second in line. The first team to make a certain number of baskets—say, five to seven—and sit down in line wins. To make this game harder, choose a more complicated defensive move like a jab, shot fake, and lay-up, or a jab and jump shot.

DURATION: 5 minutes.

3. 1-ON-1 CHALLENGE

Divide the players into two teams. The first players in each line stand under the basket, one on each box. The coach stands somewhere above the top of the key at the other basket. To start play, the coach rolls the ball toward the center circle, at the same time blowing the whistle to start the players off the blocks. The idea is that they will reach the center circle about the same time the ball does, so time your whistle blowing accordingly. The first person to get the ball is on offense; the other player is on defense to start. Play is now live and continues one-on-one until one of the players makes a basket. Whoever scores gets a point. That pairing sits down, and the next two in line play. If you have even lines, mix up the lines after the first run-through so the players don't always have the same partner. The winner is the first person to score five points.

DURATION: 5–8 minutes.

CHAPTER 8

THE ART OF DEFENSE

Defense is one of the hardest aspects of basketball to teach to young players, because it's something hardly any of them want to do. It's not flashy, it's not alluring, it's not highlight-film material. And it requires kids to change their ideas on what they thought was the goal of their time on the court—making baskets. Now they have to add the concept of guarding another person and preventing baskets, and doing this within the constraints of the game.

So to be a good teacher of defense, a coach has to be a good motivator. A standard reminder for older players is, "Offense wins games; defense wins championships"—but let's trust that this won't mean too much to your second graders, nor would you especially want it to. What you *can* impress upon your young players is that at some point in their basketball-playing careers, good offensive players who can't play defense will find themselves on the bench because they can't guard the opponent. Older players can begin to understand that even if they made several baskets, if they also allowed their defender to score several points and/or contribute to other points with assists and rebounds, their overall contribution to the team is greatly diminished. Defense is the rudder that helps the ship stay on course.

To better understand how to give your team a strong defensive foundation, defense can be broken into subsets: transition defense, individual defense, and team defense.

⬤ **Transition defense** is the skill of converting from offense to defense quickly. This occurs when the team on offense's shot is attempted and made; attempted and missed and the other team gets the rebound; or on a turnover when the team on defense gets the ball through a steal or through the ball going out-of-bounds off the offensive team.

⬤ **Individual defense** is each player's ability to guard an offensive player from the other team, both when that player has the ball and when that player doesn't have the ball.

⬤ **Team defense** is when the five players on the team work in unison so that in addition to playing their one-on-one game, at any given time during the game four other players are supporting the player who is guarding the ball.

To teach what to do after the team on offense misses a shot or turns over the ball, coaches can use the following progression, depending upon the experience and ability level of the team:

A.   Run back to a spot at the other end of the court.
B.   Run back and find the person they're guarding.
C.   Run back and identify the open person, who the biggest threat is, and who needs to be guarding

For Group I, working on A—a rudimentary zone defense—is enough to get started. For Group II, focus on B—understanding, consistency, and competency in guarding their man. Experienced teams in Group III can work on C, the nuances of defense that will allow them during the game to make some of their own decisions in the overall scheme of guarding their basket.

In order to make this transition as smooth and effective as possible, you as a coach want to encourage your players in all age groups to do three things:

1.   Sprint back to the paint around the opponent's basket to protect the basket.
2.   Stop the ball, making sure the offense doesn't get into the paint with the ball.
3.   Communicate while they find a man, remembering that in transition they must find *a* man, not necessarily their man.

Defensive Drills

Transition Defense

1. CONVERSION DRILL

Set up your team in a scrimmage situation with five players on offense and five on defense. Have the team on offense dribble the ball in and shoot a lay-up. As soon as the shot is taken, yell something like "Sprint back," or "Retreat back to the paint," which can later be shortened to "Back" as your players began to understand the conversion process. At this command, the team that started on offense and shot the ball is to sprint back to the other basket and get into positions in the paint (see the diagram on page 95). The team that was on defense either gets the rebound or, if the shot went in, a player steps out-of-bounds and throws the ball in to a teammate. This team, now on offense, dribbles down and takes a shot. The coach yells the command again, and now this team must run down to the opposite end of the court and get in the paint, in position to defend their basket. During this drill, the coach can stop and explain and help the children space themselves within the paint.

> **DURATION:** 5 minutes.

2. TWO-LINE CONVERSION DRILL

Four players are spread out evenly across the baseline, facing the court. Four other players are spread out on the foul line extended, facing the basket. The coach is at the top of the key. The coach throws the ball to the team on the baseline, which takes off, dribbling and passing toward the basket at the other end of the floor. When the ball is thrown, the foul-line players have to sprint to the basket first and get their foot in the paint. These four players then look for whom they're going to pick up to guard, finding their man or who's open. The four offensive players are trying to get a shot, and continue to pass and dribble until they shoot. Once they shoot, the teams convert again, with the team that just shot now sprinting down to the opposite end, getting one foot in the paint, selecting whom they're going to guard. After these two groups go back and forth two or three times, other players can rotate in. If you have 10 kids at practice, just substitute; if you have 12 kids, you can have three teams of 4, so one team can go off the floor and another team can rotate in.

> **STEP IT UP:** As you throw the ball to one of the players on the baseline, call out the name of someone on the foul-line team. The rest of the foul-line team sprints back while the person whose name was called has to run forward to the baseline, touch it, then sprint back to the paint and join teammates on defense. As the four come down to make a basket, the three on defense have to get in position and communicate to be able to cover the four offensive players until their other player gets back.
>
> **DURATION:** 5–10 minutes.

3. CHANGE DRILL

Set up your team with five players on offense and five players on defense on one end of the floor. Offense has the ball and begins passing and dribbling and trying to make a shot. The coach yells "Change!" and all the players on offense become defense and spring to the paint at the other end of the basket. The player guarding the person who had the ball picks up the ball; this player and team are now on offense. They dribble and pass down to the other end of the court and attempt to make a shot, and the drill continues.

> **STEP IT UP:** If you have offensive plays, work on those at the same time you're teaching conversion.
>
> **DURATION:** 5–10 minutes.

4. CONVERSION FROM REBOUND

Set up with five players on offense: the two biggest players (4, 5) on the boxes; the next biggest on the foul line (3); and the two smallest players on the corners (1, 2). Match five defenders to these players. Start the ball with player 1, who throws to 3, who throws to 2. Defensive players are moving and adjusting their positions to follow the ball movement. Player 2 shoots the ball, and 1 and 2 sprint to the other end of the court. Players

3, 4, and 5 attempt to get the rebound. The defensive players guarding 3, 4, and 5 box out (block their player's path to the basket), and the defensive players guarding 1 and 2 look out for rebounding a long shot. After the shot has gone in or the defense has retrieved the ball, players 3, 4, and 5 from both teams sprint back to the paint also. For very young players, you can stop the drill and restart it again at the other end. For older players, let the drill move up and back one or two times, like a game, before stopping, rotating other players in, and continuing.

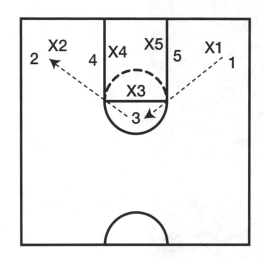

DURATION: 5 minutes.

Individual Defense

1. DEFENSIVE STANCE

This is why most players do not want to play defense. Staying in a defensive stance all the time is the only way to truly be prepared for whatever moves an opponent is going to make, either with or without the ball. Defense is about readiness and balance. Defensive stance means a player is down low, his feet shoulder width apart, balanced on the balls of his feet, his knees bent, his back straight, his hands held up and open between his waist and chest. This position gives the player the best chance at guarding someone who's moving forward while he himself is moving backward and sidewise. The offensive player knows where he's going; the defensive player's objective is to stop him. To practice this stance, have your team line up on the court and take this stance. Give individual comments to each player to ensure the correct position. Start with the team holding the stance for 10 seconds at a time and increase as they learn the position and can hold it longer.

Set up for defensive stance, dominant foot forward.

Defensive stance.

DURATION: 5 minutes.

2. WAVE DRILL FOR DEFENSIVE FOOTWORK

Have the team spread out over the half court in a defensive stance—knees bent, dominant foot slightly forward, hands up around chest level. They are going to stay in this stance while they come forward, go backward, or go from side to side, taking rapid or sliding steps while they stay crouched. To start, yell "Defense, slide!" and point a specific direction. Then, "Defense, slide!" and point another direction. For Group I, the mini sessions in each direction can be 15 seconds long; Group II can do 20 seconds; Group III can do 30 seconds. This drill builds muscles while teaching your players to maintain a defensive stance and use the appropriate footwork while changing directing.

STEP IT UP: Add three more options for the mini sessions: "Rebound!" means they all have to jump up as if going for a ball; "Loose ball!" means they all have to dive on the floor; and "Fast break!" means they all have to sprint forward.

DURATION: 3–5 minutes.

3. SLIDE DRILL

Three players are lined up in the center of the paint: one just in front of the basket, one at the foul line, one in between, all in defensive stance. The coach, standing in front of them, points either left or right. The three players slide to the edge of the foul lane in the direction pointed, then to the other edge of the foul lane, back and forth a few times as the coach points to change direction. Then next three players rotate in.

DURATION: 5 minutes.

4. T-DRILL

Players line up along the baseline facing the court with the beginning of the line under the basket. Player A starts in defensive stance under the basket and slides forward to center court, then slides backward to the foul line, then slides sideways to the sideline and sideways back to the other sideline, then jogs back to the end of the line as player B starts the drill. With two baskets, this drill can be going on at both ends of the court.

STEP IT UP: When A reaches the middle of the T, B starts the drill. Soon there are several players running the drill so the players have to talk to each other, call out where they're going, put their hands out, and guide themselves around each other.

DURATION: 5 minutes.

5. ZIGZAG DRILL

Player A starts on the baseline in the corner, facing away from the court. In defensive stance, she slides on a diagonal to the closest elbow. Now, to change direction, she executes a drop step in defensive stance. This is accomplished by taking her top foot and, with the momentum of the same side's arm and elbow, swinging back to open her body and prepare to move in an opposing direction. Player B can now start at the beginning while A slides diagonally out to the hash mark on the sideline, then into the center circle, out to the next hash mark, into the elbow, ending up in the corner opposite where she started, to walk or jog down the sideline to the end of the line. Player C has started when B reached the first elbow, and so forth. Cones can be used instead of the floor markings. The drill can be running with lines on both sides of the court.

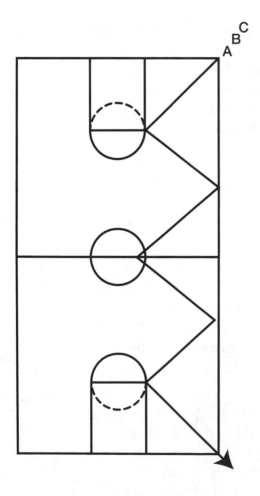

STEP IT UP: Have the team do this drill with hands behind their backs. Then they can do the drill as partners, one dribbling and one staying with the ball handler as if on defense, starting slowly at first and then speeding up.

DURATION: 5–10 minutes.

6. FLAT TRIANGLE DRILL

An understanding of guarding "off the ball"—guarding players who do not have the basketball—is critical to building a team's defense. Most players, younger or older, tend to relax and at times not concentrate when their player does not have the ball. This is a mistake and fatal to good defense. Players guarding a defender without a ball must maintain a defensive stance, be alert, and maintain vision of the basketball so that they're prepared for moves such as reversal of the ball back to their player, cuts to the basket, screens, and rebounds.

This drill introduces the concept of "ball–you–man." A beginning basketball player must learn to maintain a relationship between the player with the ball, the defender (himself), and the player he's guarding. This is often described as a flat triangle. The base of the triangle is the line from player A (with the ball) to player B. Defending player C, who is guarding B, maintains a relationship a few steps off that line and uses his peripheral vision to see both the man with the ball and the man he is guarding, forming the top of the triangle.

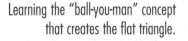
Learning the "ball-you-man" concept that creates the flat triangle.

For this drill, start with three players on the court. Player A can be at the foul line extended on the right side, B can be on the foul line extended on the left side, and defender C can be in the middle of the lane. Start by having A roll the ball to B to identify the line. C is in ready position a few steps off the line, head facing forward to see both A and B peripherally. Have C raise his arms and point to A and B so the trio can identify the flat triangle. B rolls the ball back to A and goes to a different place on the floor. C needs to readjust himself accordingly. A rolls the ball to B, and again C checks position and points at A and B. Rotate one player off and another player on the court from the waiting line and continue the drill.

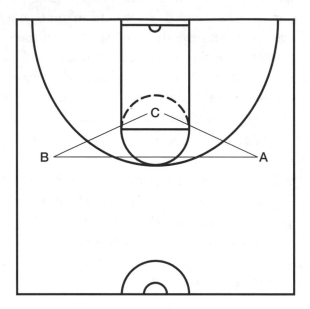

STEP IT UP: Player A has the ball, with players B and C in position as above. This time, instead of rolling the ball to B, A can begin dribbling and moving with C adjusting position; or B can cut to the basket with C repositioning to make the flat triangle.

DURATION: 10–15 minutes.

7. POST DEFENSE

One of the most dangerous areas on the basketball court to defend is what's referred to as the low post. The low post is the area 5 feet from the basket, whether on the blocks or in the paint. If an offensive player catches the ball in this area, it puts a lot of pressure on the defense because these are high-percentage shooting areas. It is extremely important for a young player to learn the skills and techniques to keep the ball out of this area. The three basic ways to play an offensive player on the low post are as follows:

A. **Play behind.** To spend a lot of time teaching how to play behind the post is only acceptable if you're coaching Shaq. Playing defense from behind always puts that player in a good rebounding position, but it also sets the defender up to be called for a foul when reaching in or over the player being guarded. It can be used if you have a tall player and can take advantage of an extreme height differential, but young players need to understand other ways.

B. **Play in front.** Using the technique of fronting the post, the defender gets her whole body in front of the offensive player, with her hands up in the air and her backside against the body of the player she's defending so she can know which way the defender's moving. The downside here is that the offensive player is in a better position to get the rebound, so when the ball goes up, the player on defense must immediately spin off and behind to get in a better position for the rebound.

C. **Three-quartering the post.** The best compromise for the young player is to "three-quarter" the post, a position where the defending player is not behind or in front of the player he's guarding, but somewhere on the side that the ball is on, just slightly to the front.

Players 1, 2, and 3 are on offense for this drill that teaches three-quartering the post. Player 1 is above the top of the key to the right, 2 is below the foul line extended, and 3 is at the low post. Player 4 is three-quartering the post on the baseline side. Players 1 and 2 pass back and forth once or twice, while 3 follows and moves into position to receive the ball, and 4 keeps maintaining a three-quarter position. Switch to other side and do the same thing, then rotate, taking 4 out, putting in a new 1, and continuing the drill.

DURATION: 5–7 minutes.

Three-quartering the post.

Team Defense

1. 1-ON-1 DEFENSE

The first step toward building a team defense is proficiency in guarding the ball one-on-one. Three players on offense are positioned as follows: on top of the key, on the foul line extended right side, and on the foul line extended left side. Three defensive players are guarding, one to each man on offense; their goal is to work on staying in front and moving their feet to angle their body to cut off each opponent's angle to the basket.

The player on the top of the key starts with the ball, and the drill goes "live" with the offensive man dribbling to make a shot while the defenders work on preventing the shot. The pair on the right side takes a turn, followed by the pair on the left side. The pairs rotate to the next position and the drill continues. Give all players get a chance to play offense and defense.

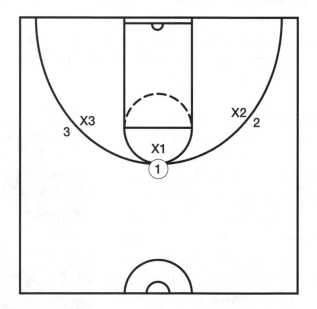

STEP IT UP: Make it harder, and more realistic, by limiting the number of dribbles—say, two or three—to get the players into good positions to pass quickly and make a basket.

DURATION: 10 minutes.

2. 2-ON-2 CLOSEOUT DRILL

Closing out is one of the hardest defensive skills, requiring skill, balance, and toughness. If a defender closes out her player's route to the basket too hard, or tight, the player will drive right by; not hard enough, and the player can shoot right over her; off balance, and she won't be able to move fast enough to follow her player's movement with the ball.

Player 1 is outside the paint on one side defended by player x1. Player 2 is on the opposite side defended by player x2. To start the drill, the coach throws the ball to player 1, who catches the ball and takes up the triple-threat position. Players x1 and x2 are in ready position, with player x2 jumping off her defender to come into the middle to form a flat triangle. Player 1 throws the ball back to the coach, who now throws the ball to 2. Player x2 comes in from the help position to guard the ball, and x1 sprints to the help position, forming the top of a flat triangle. When coach yells "Live!" whichever player has the ball goes one-on-one, dribbles, and tries to get a basket.

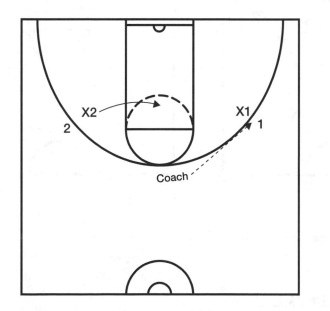

DURATION: 10 minutes.

3. 3-ON-3 DEFENDING CUTTERS

As the ball moves, all defenders not guarding the ball must "jump to the ball" by getting off their men and moving to make flat triangles. Players 1 and defender x1 are above the foul line; players 2 and x2 and 3 and x3 are on either side of the court off the elbow. Player 1 throws the ball to 2 and then cuts to the basket. Player 1x makes a flat triangle, getting behind 1 and positioning to block a pass; 3x is also making a flat triangle following the ball. If 1 gets open, 2 throws to 1 and 1 makes a basket. Alternatively, 3 has come to the top to take 1's position; 2 can throw to 3, who can then throw to 1. If 1 hasn't gotten open, 1 circles back out as 3 cuts to the basket to try to get open and make the shot. Player 2 moves up to the top; 1 can also throw to 2, who can throw to 3. To rotate, switch offenders to defenders and rotate in a new threesome.

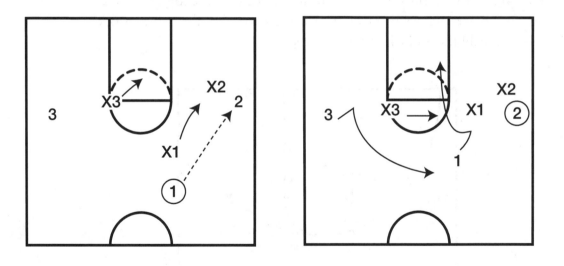

DURATION: 5–10 minutes.

4. SCREEN DRILL

A screen is when an offensive player puts his body in the way of a defender to get him off the ball, thereby freeing up his teammate to dribble or shoot. This drill has eight players, four on offense, four on defense. Player 1 has the ball, guarded by x1 at the top of the key. Players 2 and x2 are under the basket; 3 and x3 and 4 and x4 are on either elbow. To start the drill, 3 and 4 come down and screen on the boxes, screening x2. Player 2 comes off either screen on the side—and now 1 can throw the ball to 2. Player 2 catches it, faces up in the triple-threat position, then throws the ball back to 1, goes back to the middle, and the drill repeats, this time with 2 coming off the opposite side of the screen. Do this back and forth two or three times then rotate 4s out, new 1s in, and repeat the drill.

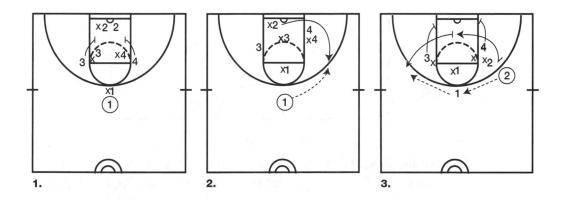

1.   2.   3.

Step It Up: When player 2 catches the ball, depending upon which side he came off, x3 or x4 has to work on post defense.

Duration: 5 minutes.

5. 4-on-4 Shell Drill

This drill works on a multitude of team defense concepts including guarding the ball, help-side/strong-side defense, and positioning in flat triangles. Players 1 and 2 are off either elbow, guarded by x1 and x2. Players 3 and 4 are off the wings, guarded by x3 and x4.

Player 1 has the ball, while x1 guards 1; x2, x3, and x4 get in position to form flat triangles, one hand pointing to the ball, the other pointing to their man. When the coach tells 1 to pass, 1 passes to 3. As the pass is being made, x1, x2, and x4 move into flat triangle position and point to the ball and their man again. Then 3 passes back to 1; then 1 to 2; then 2 to 4; each time the off-ball players are moving into position and pointing to ball and man. Rotate by pairs to the next position.

STEP IT UP: When one of the players is holding the ball, the coach can call "Drive." The player with the ball drives down the middle or to the baseline with a couple of dribbles while the other players move again to position themselves to stop the ball. The next step would be to have the coach yell "Live," and the offense, while staying in basically the same positions, can pass, dribble once or twice, and attempt to make a basket while the defense attempts to stop the ball.

DURATION: 10–20 minutes.

Games

1. DEFENSIVE KNOCKOUT

Player A stands in front of the basket in the center of the paint, facing player B who stands in front of the foul line in the center of the paint. The rest of the team lines up behind the foul line. The coach chooses the boundaries that the players are going to slide to by placing cones or tape Xs equidistant on both sides of both players. The players take a defensive stance, and the coach blows the whistle or yells "Go." Players stay low and slide first to one side and then to the other, the winner being the first one to touch 10 cones (for younger players this can be a lower number, or the cones can be closer). The winner stays to play again, the opponent goes to the end of the line, and the next person in line comes up to challenge the previous winner. Once a player is eliminated or knocked out twice, she sits down on the baseline or sideline and is out. The winner is the one left in. A variation, and a way to keep all the contestants honest and in defensive stance, is to hold a large bedsheet to tent the area where the players are sliding. If a player straightens up out of defensive stance and hits the bedsheet, the other player automatically wins that round.

DURATION: 5–8 minutes.

2. DEFENSIVE STOPS

This is a half-court mini scrimmage with a twist: The only way a team gets a point is through defense. Set up two teams of three, four, or five players each using pinneys or some other method to distinguish the teammates. You can flip for who starts; the team winning the flip would start without the ball. The team on offense is trying to score; the team on defense is trying to get the ball. Anytime the team on defense steals or rebounds to secure possession, they get a point and remain on defense. The team on offense benefits from making a basket as quickly as possible because then possession will change, and they will have an opportunity to be on defense and begin accruing points. Divide your group into three even teams and you can have a mini tournament, or use two larger teams and sub in if necessary.

DURATION: 5–8 minutes.

CHAPTER 9

THE ART OF REBOUNDING

Coaches want rebounders, at the defensive and offensive end of the court, and there are two reasons why.

First, a team can never be great defensively unless they can rebound. If a shot goes up from the offensive side and the other team cannot get a high number of rebounds, that team, in many ways, has wasted all the energy and strategy that went into playing defense. If your team can "control the glass," however—get the rebound and pass back out to a player who can then make a fast break—they have now given themselves the easiest opportunity to make a good shot. You'll have opportunities for lay-ups, two-on-one situations, and free throws.

The second reason is the high percentage of baskets made on second or third shots after grabbing an offensive rebound off a first shot. "If you were to chart the percentage of shots made from offensive rebounds, the rise is astronomical," says Coach Carroll. "An average shot percentage of 50 percent for your team in a game is good. But an average shot percentage for second and third shots will generally run between 60 and 70 percent." Those second and third attempts are also much more likely to draw a foul, which may result in free throws. Allowing opposing teams second and third shots is devastating and can cause you to lose many games.

The team that controls the boards controls the game. A coach of young players wants to always teach and stress the importance of rebounding at both ends of the floor.

Relentless Pursuit of the Ball

Rebounding has been described as 75 percent effort and determination and 25 percent skill and technique. There are many excellent rebounders who aren't the tallest players on the court. What great NBA rebounders, such as Dennis Rodman and Ben Wallace, do have in common is relentless effort in going to the glass at both ends of the floor and getting the ball. In fact, *great rebounders look at every shot attempt as a pass to themselves.* That mind-set is probably as important to getting rebounds as any other single factor. *Relentless pursuit of the ball is what makes great rebounders.*

Several other aspects that you can help your players acquire contribute to the ability to rebound. Crucial is anticipating where the ball is going to go. This comes from a focus on seeing the ball, from becoming aware of where each teammate is most likely to shoot, from learning to turn, move, and pivot in ways that allow constant eye contact with the ball. Balance is important, too, because it allows the player to jump, go left, go right, go forward, quickly. Quickness in moving the feet and rotating the torso also aids the rebounder, as do strength and jumping ability.

 **EXPERIENCE TALKS:** One of the best ways to improve jumping ability is by jumping: trying to touch the net, the backboard, the rim. As players get older, it is important for them to develop back, shoulder, and leg strength for rebounding. This can be done with weight training and coaching tools like strength shoes.

The technique of teaching rebounding can be broken down into six components.

1. Use a verbal command of "See" to remind your players constantly that as soon as the shot goes up, the essence of rebounding is seeing and computing where that ball is going to go.

2. Use the verbal command of "Hands" to remind your players to have their hands up. This is not only critical for rebounding but also a great aid in keeping the body balanced evenly, which will allow quicker movement in any direction. You can point out to any recalcitrant player that in the entire history of basketball, not one rebound has ever come up from the floor.

3. When the shot goes up, a player wants to move from the ball–you–man flat triangle position to basket–you–man, which is a straight-line configuration that puts her directly in the line of passage of her player going to the basket.

4. Then the player wants to make body contact, boxing out his player without losing sight of the ball.

5. Now go for the ball! Make sure your players are propelling themselves forward and upward at the same time, like an airplane, not just upward like a helicopter.

6. To truly complete the defensive rebound, the player finishes with a quick pivot and an outlet pass to a perimeter teammate. The receiving player can advance to a fast break and make the basket.

Drills

1. REBOUNDING AGILITY

Set up your team at the baseline in three lines with one line between the foul lane and sideline, one line in the middle of the foul lane, and one line between the foul line and other sideline. The first person in each line starts with her hands up and begins running V-cuts, taking two or three steps in one direction, then two or three steps in another direction. Once she starts her second V, the next person in line can start. Players can do this to the half-court line, or full court, and come back. Next, each starting player has a ball. She dribbles to the foul line or foul line extended, pivots, passes the ball back to the next person in line, then sprints back, changing direction every couple of steps.

In the next sequence, the player runs with her hands up on a hard drive to the foul line, stops with a jump stop, then pivots 360 degrees, first by pivoting 180 degrees, then another 180 degrees. She then runs to half court with her hands up, jump-stops, does the pivot sequence; This is repeated at the other foul line, and at the baseline, so each player does this sequence four times.

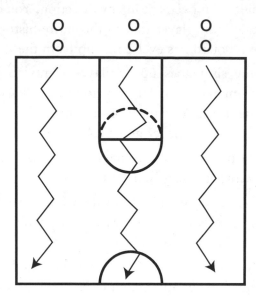

For the last sequence, the player turns sidewise and does a defensive slide to the foul line, then sprints forward to the half-court line, slides to the next foul line, and sprints to the baseline; she then can return the length of the court with the same sequence.

DURATION: 8–10 minutes.

2. TAP DRILL

Have a line facing the backboard on the right side. Group I will do this drill against a wall; they aren't tall enough to tap the ball back up against the glass. The first person in line throws the ball up against the backboard, then peels out and to the back of the line, while the next person in line moves up into position and taps the ball back up against the backboard. Players can do this on the right side using their right hand, then move the line to the left and run through the drill again with their left hand.

DURATION: 3–5 minutes.

3. LINE BOX OUT

Divide the team into two lines facing each other about a step apart somewhere on the court. One line is offense; the other line is defense. The offensive line is in shooting position; balls are not necessary, because these players are not actually going to shoot. The defensive line is in defensive stance with one hand up ready to challenge the offensive players' shot. When the coach yells "Shot," each offensive player pretends to shoot the ball. Each defensive player challenges the shot with his hand, and then performs a box out. This is done by placing a foot in front of the middle of the player being guarded, and then pivoting 180 degrees to have his back to the player and his eyes to the ball. The defensive player then makes contact by putting his lower body and back in contact with the offensive player's body behind him. Now when the offensive player moves, the defensive player will feel his motion, and move with him.

Do this sequence a few times, watching the players' techniques as they box out. Then switch and let the offensive line play defense.

STEP IT UP: When you yell "Shot," let the offense take one step; you then call out whether they'll go right or left, so the defense first challenges the shot, then has to box out the offensive player who is moving one step to the left or right. In the next progression, you yell "Shot" and each offensive player moves left or right, deciding for himself; this way, the defensive player doesn't know which way the player will go, but still has to move to box him out. For even more of a challenge, have the offensive person take one or two dribbles before shooting; the defense has to challenge the shot and then box out.

DURATION: 5 minutes.

4. THREE-MAN TIP-IN

Set up the drill with player 1 on the right side of the basket, 2 on the left side of the basket, and 3 behind 1. Player 1 puts the ball up against the backboard, "tipping" it off the tops of her fingers, so it goes over the top of the basket and comes down on the other side. As she finishes the tip, she moves quickly to the other side, ending up above 2. Player 2 than tips it back over to the other side, where 3 has moved into position. Player 2 moves quickly back over to the other side above 3, and the rotation continues, with the trio attempting to keep the ball "alive" by not missing the tip. Group I can do this drill against the wall. This drill practices jumping and also has a conditioning aspect. If you don't have enough baskets for your whole team to do the drill, rotate a second team in at both baskets as your players start to get winded.

DURATION: 3–5 minutes.

5. OUTLET PASSING

Divide your team into two groups. Line up on either elbow; each group will use their side of the half court for the drill. The first player in the line has a ball and goes to the side of the basket; the second player goes to the foul line extended, and the third player is on the foul line with a ball. All are facing the basket. The person by the rim throws the ball against the backboard, rebounds it, turns, and outlet-passes it to the player at the foul line extended. As soon as the player under the rim rebounds, the player at the foul line comes to take his position, while the rebounder takes the position of the outlet receiver and the receiver goes to the end of the line at the foul line. Then the drill repeats, continuing this three-man rotation until everyone on each side has been at every position. The lines can then switch sides and do the drill again.

STEP IT UP: Call for an increase in speed and encourage your players to move quickly to their positions and through this drill.

DURATION: 5 minutes.

6. REBOUND THE BALL

For older players in Group II, and for Group III, this is a good drill to use the Big Ball if you have one. This is an oversized heavier ball that is harder to get into the basket, so there will be more rebounds. Player A is the shooter; B is the rebounder. When A shoots the ball, B yells "Hands," putting her hands in the air and preparing to rebound. A boxes B out, gets the rebound, shoots again, and the drill continues. Player A can shoot 5 times, 10 times, or for 30 seconds; then the players rotate and B becomes the shooter. Pairs can be working on as many baskets as you have.

Boxing out for a
rebound.

7. 1-ON-1 REBOUNDING

Player A is the shooter, B is rebounding, and C is an offensive player whom B is guarding. When A shoots, B yells "Hands" and puts his hands up, then boxes out C. B gets the rebound and passes it back to A. The coach can tell C to go different places—to the elbow, toward the baseline—and B has to keep moving to get between C and the basket.

The threesome can rotate so each gets a turn at each position.

DURATION: 3–5 minutes.

8. 2-ON-2 REBOUNDING

For this drill, you can have six players at each basket. If you have additional players, rotate them in by two. Two shooters, players 1 and 2, are at each of the elbows; two offensive rebounders, 3 and 4, are just off the lane; and defensive players x3 and x4 are at the boxes. The play runs as follows: Player 1 takes a shot, x3 rebounds it and passes the ball to 2. Player 2 makes a shot, x4 rebounds it and passes it back to 1. In this drill, x3 and x4 are finding the appropriate positions depending upon whether they are help-side or strong-side rebounders. The help side is the side of the court off the basket line that does not have the ball in play; the strong side is the side of the court where the ball is in play. Play for about a minute, then rotate by pairs.

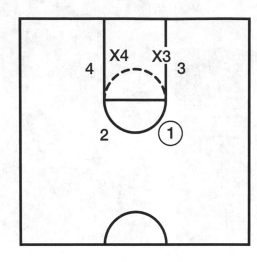

DURATION: 3–5 minutes.

9. HELP-SIDE REBOUNDING

The hard part of rebounding is that many times a player is not standing next to the player she is guarding, but rather in the help-side position. The help-side position refers to being off her man in the flat triangle configuration. If a shot is taken while a player is in the help-side position, she must expend tremendous effort to get back to her man and box her out because if her man is a good rebounder, this player is already in motion headed toward the rim. It's extremely important that this help-side player get back and make contact with her man outside the paint, or her man will have the advantage.

Set up with offensive player 1 guarded by x1 on the one wing between the elbow and hash mark. The coach is in the same general area in the other wing, with passer P at the top of the key. The rest of the team can be lined up a few steps behind the passer.

For the drill, P passes the ball to the coach, which means x1 has to move into a flat triangle position. Then coach yells "Shot" and shoots, at which point x1 needs to get back and box out 1 before 1 gets to the paint. So x1 runs back to stop 1 by putting an arm or leg in her way, then pivoting, sitting down low with her backside against 1, and then moving with 1 as 1 tries to get into the paint.

To rotate, P becomes 1; 1 becomes x1; x1 goes out; and a new P comes in from the line.

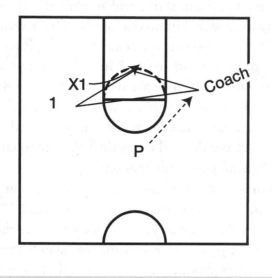

DURATION: 5 minutes.

10. MOVE DRILL

This drill teaches players how to stay in stance, move, and then react to boxing out as the shot is taken.

Put four offensive players on the perimeter, two right above the elbows, two down low off the box, with four corresponding defensive players guarding them. The coach is around the top of the key with a ball. Every time the coach yells "Move," the defenders move one position clockwise, never knowing when the coach is going to yell "Shot." When the coach yells "Shot," and then shoots the ball, the offensive players move to get the rebound while each defensive player needs to find the closest man and box this player out, communicating with teammates if necessary. You can rotate through this drill using teams of four, offense rotating out to defense, defense sitting out, and a new team coming in for offense.

DURATION: 5 minutes.

Games

1. SURVIVOR

This is based on the television show, and for full effectiveness requires some narration by the coach, but no one needs to have seen the show to enjoy this game. To set the scene, the coach tells the players they are all on a tropical island; who wants to stay? In order to stay on the island, you have to get a rebound. If there are two coaches, you throw the ball back and forth so the ball keeps moving; with one coach, dribble around as you talk, so the kids never know exactly where the ball is going to go up from. Then you throw the ball up against the backboard, purposely missing, and the kids all go for the rebound.

Let's say Taran gets the rebound. You tell Taran that she has survived; she can go and sit down; she is still on the island. Play continues until you have five or six survivors; the rest have to leave the island. The survivors wave good-bye to those leaving the island; this group then goes down and practices shooting at the other end of the court. The second round eliminates two or three more players, to come up with three survivors. The third round eliminates one more from the island to leave two survivors. For the final round, call the team back and they all watch while the last two challenge each other to find out who the final survivor will be.

DURATION: 8–10 minutes.

2. CIRCLE BOX OUT

Put three or four players around the outside of the center jump circle or foul-line circle on the court. Put a corresponding three or four players on the inside of the circle, with a ball in the middle. If you have 12 players for practice, you can make three teams of 4. Players on the inside need to keep their man out for three seconds. (When a shot is taken, if a player can tie up his man for three seconds, in a game situation that player has probably prevented his player from getting a rebound.) So when the coach yells "Shot" to indicate that the shot is going up, the outside players go right or left and attempt to get in the circle and grab the ball. In order to prevent this, each inside player is going to step to the middle of his man's body, pivot, to get the player "on his back," then sit into the player, with arms up, and continue to move and change direction as that other player moves to prevent him from getting to the ball. The coach can count one–one thousand, two–one thousand, three–one thousand, or time with a stopwatch.

If the players are still basically outside the circle at the end of three seconds, the inside team gets the point. If they've made it in to touch the ball, the outside team gets the point. Or you could say that anytime an outside player gets both feet planted inside the circle, that team gets a point. If someone gets in to touch the ball, that's two points. To rotate, the inside team sits down, the outside team rotates in, the new team takes the outside team's place, and the contest continues, running a cycle of three times, or more if necessary, to get a winning team.

DURATION: 5–7 minutes.

CHAPTER 10

THE DISCIPLINE OF AGILITY AND SPEED

The ability of young basketball players to push beyond their comfort zone to achieve successive levels in their game is vital. Nowhere is this more important than in the area of agility and speed. "This can be one of the biggest pitfalls for young players," says Coach Carroll. "For each new level that the young player rises to in his or her game, the most significant difference is speed." But speed and agility are things that can be developed at a young age, so players never have to allow this to be a determining factor as to whether they can play the game of basketball.

Coaches also want to avoid a common pitfall, says Toronto Raptors strength and conditioning coach Shawn Brown. "It's a mistake to think agility and speed drills are the same as conditioning drills. They are not the same. When doing agility and speed drills, you don't want tongues hanging and players out of breath. Agility is the ability to change direction quickly. You want to practice agility drills fresh."

In teaching kids speed and agility, a lot of what you as a coach are doing is teaching the kids how to move. According to Coach Brown, physical education teachers don't necessarily teach kids how to move. And in fact, most NBA players have never been taught how to move.

The advantage of teaching such techniques to a younger audience is that they love to move, all over the place, and will likely take to these drills with much more enthusiasm than a practice group of NBA players.

Mechanics for Speed

For these drills, use the following mechanics for speed to help your players get the most out of their practice.

Start in a good two-point stance, or ready position, with feet shoulder width apart, knees bent, weight balanced. Coach Brown suggests that kids may be more comfortable in this stance with their nondominant foot slightly forward.

For speed, the major point to remember at this stage is that the kids need enough of a leg lift to let the foot drop so that the toe extends toward the ground. This lets the foot land and then recoil to spring into the next stride. A way to teach this to your players is to make sure they lift their knees high enough that their thigh is roughly parallel with the ground.

Leg high enough to let foot drop and toe extend; arms pumping straight.

The upper body is leaning slightly forward. The arms are bent and pump "eyebrow to back pocket"—fingertips up to the level of the eyebrows, returning to the back pocket. The arms swing front and back—never across in front or behind the body, because this slows the runner down. Kids should pick a spot to focus on, keeping their head facing straight ahead.

Drills

1. Agility and Speed Warm-Up

For this warm-up, divide your team into two groups and line the first group up on the baseline. Start by jogging to the other baseline and back; then the second group does the same thing. The series continues as follows:

- Sprint three-quarters of the court to the opposite foul line extended and back.

ⓘ   Slide sideways up and back.

ⓘ   Backpedal, running backward up and back.

As an alternative warm-up, use individual jump ropes and have your team do some regular jumping, high-stepping, and fast jumping.

DURATION: 5 minutes.

2. STRETCHING

After a light warm-up drill or some jumping rope, you can do a stretch with your team. Younger players are generally not focused on stretching, because their bodies tend to be much more limber, but you as a coach may want to help your young players get into this habit for their later years. As kids approach the growth period of adolescence, their body enters a period of less flexibility, becomes more flexible during the late-teen years, and then decreases in flexibility again in the early twenties. Stretching does help prevent injuries and makes a person more flexible and therefore more athletic.

A basic stretch series for basketball will consist of 8 to 10 stretches, mostly of the big core muscles with some simple arm movements. Coach Brown prefers the control of a stable stretch—holding the stretch for 30 seconds, then releasing for 2 to 3 seconds, then holding again—as opposed to a dynamic or bouncing stretch.

1.   With legs apart, bend over and put the hands on the floor in a standing V, then walk the hands over to stretch to the left side and then to the right.

2.   From the same standing position, legs apart, bend one knee and lunge to the left side, then to the right.

3.   From a standing position, go into a full, deep squat, like a baseball catcher's position.

4.   Sitting, put the legs out in a V and stretch forward to the middle, then to the left, then to the right.

5.   Sitting, stick the legs out straight in front, together, with the toes straight up, and touch the ankles or toes.

6. Lie on one side and grab the skyward leg, pulling the heel to the rear end for a quadriceps stretch. Then stretch the other side.

7. Sitting, put the soles of the feet together in a yoga position, then push down on the thighs and lean forward for a groin stretch.

8. Standing, lunge forward on one knee with the back foot flat to feel a calf stretch in the back leg; switch legs and repeat.

9. With the arms extended, do some arm circles forward and backward.

10. Reach to the sky with one arm, then bend to touch between the shoulder blades while pulling down on the elbow; switch sides and repeat.

DURATION: 10 minutes.

3. HAND DRILL

This is a reactionary agility drill where players have to focus on the coach and move as a response to the coach's movements.

The players spread out on the half court and take a defensive or ready position facing the coach. When you raise your left hand, they slide to the right; you then raise your right hand and they slide to the left; or you can use one hand and point back and forth. Another method would be to have a tennis ball in each hand. Whichever hand you use to throw the ball up, the players have to slide toward that side. Have the players sliding hard for 15 to 30 seconds, then resting for 15 seconds, then hard again for 15 to 30 seconds; do three or four sets.

STEP IT UP: A variation on this drill has the players pairing up, taking turns being the leader and then the follower.

DURATION: 3 minutes.

4. Foot-Fire Drill

This drill teaches players to move their feet quickly, and also includes a conditioning component. Have your team spread out over the half court and take a defensive stance. Upon command, or a blow of the whistle, they start by running in place, their feet just inches off the ground, as fast as possible, 15 seconds on, 15 seconds off, and so on, over time working up to one-minute-on, one-minute-off sequencing. You can also include a "Rebound" command, at which the kids have to repeatedly jump up, going for that rebound.

STEP IT UP: Players spread out on the half court and, using the boundary line of the court, with one foot on either side, foot-fire forward moving around the court. Or do the drill moving laterally over the sideline around the court.

DURATION: 2–3 minutes.

5. Hop Drill

This drill was made famous by NBA player Mark Eaton, who at 7 feet, 4 inches had the height he needed but initially not the footwork. Mark five spots on the floor in the configuration of a big X. In the manner of hopscotch, players can start on their right foot at one leg of the X and hop to the middle, then to the top of that leg, then over to the top of the other leg, then to the middle again, then down to the bottom. Then do the figure again hopping only on the left foot; then hopping with both feet. Finish by separating the feet to cover both legs, then hop together with both feet on the center, then separate to hop on the top of the X legs, then, without turning around, hop backward.

DURATION: 3–5 minutes.

6. MIRROR DODGE DRILL

For this drill, you can set up two cones 8 to 10 yards apart, or designate a similar-sized area on the court. Players pair up (you will have six or seven pairs at the most) and position themselves in defensive stance an arm length apart in the area designated by the two cones, facing each other. When the coach blows the whistle, the offensive player makes as many moves as he can to attempt to get by the defense; the defense tries to stay with him. One option for this drill is to position yourself so the players designated as offense can see you and then indicate what moves they should take—sprinting, sliding to the left, sliding to the right, backpedaling. The defense cannot see you so they will have to follow without knowing what's coming next.

> **STEP IT UP:** For older players, tell them beforehand the different moves they need to include in their sequence, and then let them decide when and where to use the moves.
>
> **DURATION:** 3 minutes.

Games

1. SIMON SAYS

This is an absolute favorite, especially with the younger kids. It's fun, and requires extreme focus and both quickness of thinking and movement even with just the regular commands—"Put your hand on your head," "Bend your knees," "Clap once," et cetera. To review, the coach stands in front of the team, facing the team. Anytime the coach says "Simon says" before a command, the players are to do that command: "Simon says put your hands on your head." But anytime the leader just gives a command, "Bend your knees," without the "Simon says," all those who bend their knees are out and go sit down. The winner is the last player standing. One variation would be to let this child come up front and take a turn as leader.

To make this game more basketball oriented, add some of these commands: "Get in defensive stance," followed by "Go forward," "Go backward," "Go sideways," "Shot" (put a hand up to deflect a shot),

"Rebound" (hands up and jump), "Take a charge" (fall backward), "Loose ball" (dive to the floor), "Sprint," and "Foot fire."

2. OBSTACLE AND RELAY COURSES

Few youngsters can resist obstacle and relay courses, and it's a great way to give your team some relaxed fun yet still practice worthwhile skills.

Here are a few variations; you or your team can come up with some of your own regional favorites.

- A simple relay is to divide the team in two and have them line up at the baseline on either side of the basket. The object is for every player to sprint down to the other end of the court, make a lay-up, sprint back, and go sit down at the end of the line. When the coach blows the whistle, the relay starts. The first team to be finished and sitting wins.

- Here's a relay course best done outdoors with water that stretches the kids' dribbling skills. Mark a course on the court with cones, markers, bases, or chalk or tape. Divide your players into two teams, and position the teams at opposite corners of the court. Each team starts with a Dixie cup full of water. The first player dribbles along the baseline to the other end with the cup in one hand, dribbling with the other, then switches hands to come back. She then either passes the cup off or has to pour the water from her cup into the cup of the next player in line, while both are dribbling. The goal is to keep as much water in the cup as possible. This could also be done as individuals, timed, to see who can get the fastest time dribbling up and back with the most water in the cup. Indoors, the cup can be filled with confetti.

- Another option—popular at NBA halftimes—is to have a race where the kids put on a big shirt and big shorts, and dribble to the end and back. This can be done as teams, with each player sitting down at the end of the line when finished. The team with everyone seated first wins.

- To challenge the dribbling skills of older children, divide your players into two teams. Then each team divides their players so that half are on the baseline and half are at half court, or full court, depending upon their ages. The first player is blindfolded with an Ace bandage and has to dribble down to his team player at the other end without being able to see the ball. The blindfold is transferred to the next player and the relay continues. A variation is to have the coach call out the dribble, left-handed, right-handed, or stop— where they have to dribble in place before the coach indicates they can continue.

Part III

ESSENTIAL INFORMATION

RULES OF BASKETBALL

As mentioned in the beginning, this book presumes that by deciding to coach a basketball team, you have an interest in the sport, and therefore some idea of how the game is played. This summary is intended as a very basic overview to aid you in your coaching of younger players. For in-depth specifics, books and Web sites are readily available with common high school basketball game rules. These can vary slightly from region to region, so find what source is being used in your area.

Beginning Basics

The game is played on a court with two baskets. Two teams with five people each are on the floor during play. The object of the game is to score the most baskets. This is achieved by putting the basket in your designated hoop when your team is on *offense* and in possession of the ball, and preventing your opponents from putting the ball in their designated hoop when they have the ball and your team is on *defense*.

In order to move the ball around the court, a player may throw, pass, or bounce the ball while walking or running. A player cannot run holding the ball and cannot kick the ball. Upon catching the ball, a player may move one foot, but not both. To walk or run with the ball, the player must dribble with one hand.

Referees manage the game, and indicate stoppage of play for violations or fouls by blowing a whistle. If two players appear to have equal possession of the ball, referees call a jump ball. In high school, teams take turns receiving possession for jump balls.

Violations

To violate these ball movement rules results in the other team gaining possession of the ball. Examples are as follows: If a player moves more than one foot without dribbling, this is a *traveling* violation. If a player dribbles with two hands, or stops and resumes dribbling, this is a *double-dribble* violation. If a player brings the ball up with a palm underneath and facing upward, this is a *carrying* violation. When a team loses control or knocks the ball out-of-bounds, the other team gets to inbound the ball. Nonfoul violations of this type result in a *turnover*—play is stopped and the other team gets the ball. Generally, when play is stopped by a referee for any reason, play resumes again by inbounding the ball. This means a player goes out-of-bounds and has five seconds to throw the ball in to a teammate.

Fouls

Holding, pushing, tripping, or striking an opponent is not permitted, and doing so to the extent that it prohibits the flow of the game is a *foul*. The referee calls a personal foul on the player committing the violation. When a player has a certain number of fouls—five in most town, school, and college leagues—that player has fouled out and cannot play anymore.

If a player fouls an opponent during the act of shooting, the opponent is awarded a free throw or throws. If the basket went in despite the foul, the team gets the points, and the player gets one free throw. If the basket didn't go in, the player gets two or three free throws, depending upon whether the player's feet were inside or outside the three-point line. A free throw is a shot taken, unguarded, from the foul line while play is stopped, and is worth one point. Remaining players can line up on either side outside the lane to attempt to get the rebound. If any player steps over the lines marking the lane before the ball hits the rim, this is a violation, and the other team gets the ball, or another shot, depending upon which team caused the violation.

Teams are also permitted only a certain number of fouls. For most school games, this is six total team fouls per half. When a team has more than this, they are *over the limit*. If they commit another foul, the opposing team is considered *in the bonus* and gets to shoot *one-and-one*. This is a free throw from the foul line. If the first shot goes in, the player gets a second shot. If the first shot is a miss, the other team gets the ball.

If a team has more than nine fouls, this is called a *double bonus* and opponents automatically get two free throws.

Time Constraints

A team has five seconds to inbound the ball after a basket, violation, or foul.

After play begins, if the team has inbounded the ball at the opponent's end of the court, they have 10 seconds to advance the ball to their half of the court. Once the ball crosses the half-court line, the team with the ball must stay on their front court. If the ball goes to the back court and is touched by one of the players on offense before it is touched by one of the players on defense, this is a *back-court violation,* and results in the ball being turned over to the other team.

The other time-controlled violation is the *three-second* rule. An offensive player cannot be in the lane for more than three consecutive seconds unless the ball is being shot. If the shot hits the rim, the clock resets, and the player now has an additional three seconds.

Operation Rules

Middle and high school basketball games generally have four 8-minute quarters or two 16-minute halves. The game begins with a center jump. The referee stands in the center of the center circle, with one player from each team on either side. The referee tosses the ball upward, and each player tries to tap it to a teammate lined up outside the circle.

Referees are the only ones who can stop the game clock. They do this for violations, fouls, or when a coach or player calls for a time-out. During play, teams can only call for a time-out if they are in possession of the ball or play is stopped. Teams are permitted a limited number of time-outs per game. Player substitutions can only be made while play is stopped. To indicate a substitution, players go to the scorer's table and wait for the referee to motion them into the game.

Basketball games cannot end with a tie. In tie situations, until college, the overtime period is generally three minutes. These overtimes will continue until an overtime ends with one team ahead.

GLOSSARY

Assist—a pass that results in the scoring of a basket.

Backboard—the board holding the basket.

Back court—the half of the court with the opponent's basket.

Back-court violation—when a team is on their half of the court, and they return to the opposing team's half of the court with the ball.

Backdoor—a cut made by an offensive player when pressured by the defense.

Backscreen—when a player positions the body, back to the rim, in the path of an opponent.

Baseline—the line on each end of the court that delineates the in-bounds and out-of-bounds areas; also called end line.

Basket—the hoop and net attached to the backboard that the ball has to go through to score.

Block—when an opponent gets a hand on just the ball on its upward arc to legally prevent it from going in the basket.

Bounce pass—a pass sent off the floor.

Box—the black boxes marked on the lane.

Box out—to block the opponent's path by using the body.

Carry—bringing the ball upward with the palm underneath; this is a violation.

Charge—when a defensive player assumes position in front of an offensive player and the offensive player knocks this defender over.

Chest pass—a pass thrown from the chest with two hands.

Clear out—teammates go to the baseline or the sides to open up the lane for the player with the ball.

Control dribble—bouncing the basketball, knees bent, low to the floor, with other arm up to protect the ball.

Crossover—using a dribble to cross the ball from one hand to the other.

Curl cut—a cut made by an offensive player coming off a screen and curling to the basket.

Cut—a change of direction by an offensive player to get open.

Defense—the team that does not have the ball and is preventing the other team from scoring.

Double dribble—dribbling the ball with two hands at the same time, or dribbling, then stopping dribbling, then dribbling again; these are violations.

Down screen—when a player positions the body, back to the basketball, in the path of an opponent.

Dribble—to bounce the basketball off the fingertips.

Drive—direct dribble to the basket.

Elbow—the corner where the foul line and painted lane meet

Fake—pretend to do a specific move to throw the defender off, and then do something else.

Fast break—when a team gets the ball and advances down the court ahead of their opponents to try for an uncontested basket.

Field goal—all baskets made except free throws.

Flash—a movement by a player away from the basketball to a clear area closer to the basketball.

Foul—when a player holds, grabs, or hits an opponent in a manner that disrupts the flow of the game.

Foul line—the line that borders the end of the painted rectangle away from the basket.

Free throw—an unguarded shot attempt from the top of the lane while play is stopped; this is awarded when the offensive team is fouled in the act of shooting.

Front court—the half of the court containing a team's basket.

Give and go—an offensive move where the give is the pass from one teammate to another, who then goes to the basket.

Half court—the half of the court on either side of the painted line through the center circle dividing the court in the middle.

Hash mark—a short line on either sideline between the foul line extended and the half-court line.

Help side—also called weak side; dividing the court longitudinally through the basket, this is the side where the ball is not in play.

Hesitation—a slowing of speed during a speed dribble to get a defender to relax.

High post—an area around the free-throw line.

Hook shot—a shot taken with one arm by hooking the hand around the ball and arcing over the head.

Hoop—another name for the basket.

In-bound pass—when a player out-of-bounds passes the ball in-bounds to resume play.

Inside—refers to a position closer to the basket than the opponent.

Jab step—a hard short step forward at the defender to create an opening to shoot or drive.

Jump ball—when the referee throws the ball up in the middle of two opponents to start or resume play.

Jump shot—a shot taken by jumping and shooting at the same time.

Key—the painted rectangle, or lane, below the basket.

Lay-up—a close, one-hand shot from either side of the basket.

Loose ball—When the ball is not in either team's possession.

Low post—the area 5 feet from the basket, whether on the blocks or in the paint.

Man—used to designate the opponent an individual player is to defend.

Offense—the team with the ball attempting to score.

One-and-one—a free-throw situation where the player has to make the first free throw in order to take a second.

Outlet pass—when a team gets the rebound and passes the ball out quickly to a perimeter player to advance the ball.

Over the limit—when a team has seven or more fouls.

Overhead pass—a pass made with two hands over the head.

Overtime—when the game ends in a tie score, this is the additional period(s) played.

Paint—the painted rectangular area on the court in front of the basket.

Pick and roll—an offensive move where a player sets a screen and then rolls the body around and goes toward the basket.

Pivot—turning on one foot to change directions.

Post up—when an offensive player assumes position close to the basket with the back to the basket.

Rebound—retrieving the ball off a missed shot.

Screen—when an offensive player puts the body in the way of a defender to get the defender off the ball.

Strong side—dividing the court longitudinally through the basket, this is the side where the ball is in play.

Stutter—taking quick low steps close to the ground.

Substitute—when a player goes into the game for another player who comes out.

Technical foul—when a player or coach does something unsportsmanlike such as using raw or derogatory language or purposely kicking the ball; it results in two free throws and possession of the ball.

Three seconds—when an offensive player remains for more than three consecutive seconds in the key; this is a violation.

Time-out—official stoppage of play.

Top of the key—the high point of the circle above the paint.

Traveling—when a player walks or runs without dribbling the ball.

Turnover—when the offensive team loses possession of the ball.

V-cut—when a player cuts in one direction, then changes direction and cuts at an angle, running a V.

Weak side—see Help side.

Wing—the area just above and below the foul line extended on either side of the court.

THE AUTHORS

Beverly   Austin   John

Beverly Breton Carroll is a freelance writer whose work, both nonfiction and fiction, has appeared in numerous magazines and newspapers throughout the United States. John Carroll, assistant coach of the Boston Celtics, was a standout player at Dickinson College in Carlisle, Pennsylvania, and is a former assistant coach at Seton Hall University in New Jersey and head coach at Duquesne University in Pittsburgh. Beverly and John and their son Austin currently live in a historic area of eastern Massachusetts, near the path of Paul Revere's midnight ride and Thoreau's Walden Pond, where Beverly occasionally gets them to do something other than basketball.

Photographer Steve Lipofsky has been the official photographer for the Boston Celtics since the 1981–1982 season. His work appears in major publications throughout the world including *Sports Illustrated, Sport, TIME* and many others.

INDEX